1ˢᵗ YEAR HUMANITIES
HOW TO EXCEL

JANET TYSON

Tripping Lightly Books
VICTORIA   BC

National Library of Canada Cataloguing in Publication Data

Tyson, Janet, 1962-
1st year humanities

Includes bibliographical references.
ISBN 0-9689912-0-3

1. Humanities--Study and teaching (Higher) 2. Study skills. 3. College student orientation. I. Title. II. Title: First year humanities.
LB2395.T97 2001 378.1'70281 C2001-911587-3
--

Cover: Alfred the Great, Winchester.
Photograph by the author.

This book is dedicated to my Mother - a teacher and friend.

Tripping lightly through Humanity
on our way to greatness...

Table of Contents

Chapter 1: A Personal Decision

My decision to write a book such as this was influenced, primarily, by two things: the memory of a first year student who had never heard of something called a "primary source" - me - and a number of my own pupils who seemed to ask similar questions regarding the analysis of English literature. Somewhere along the way, I concluded, something had been lost in the system...

I returned to my education after several years in the "world." One day, after much self-searching, I left everything, came back to Canada (from my home in England) and went straight into full-time school!

When I first applied, I had lofty ideals of becoming a scientist for NASA! I enrolled in the sciences - Physics, Chemistry, Calculus - only to find these subjects incredibly lacking in imagination and freedom. Don't get me wrong, I still love to imagine myself the scientist, and I am continuing in the goal of getting a science degree before I'm seventy-five, but it wasn't what I was looking for, I guess, so my grades reflected my disinterest and lack of passion, and I limped out of my first year with a low C+ average. This was devastating to me, as I had always *imagined* myself as an "A" student, even though, looking back on my high school grades, I only achieved "A's" in about half my courses - I pulled out of the sciences before I became disillusioned, left my NASA hopes behind me, and decided to sample the rest of the college's offerings.

First, I relished in English literature for a while, and was blessed with an excellent instructor who recognized my potential and set me up in an advanced program with another keen student. Being a relatively small college, there was time for this kind of personal attention - something I had to fight for at U.B.C., with many thousands of other students all hoping for the same thing. Immediately, my grades shot up to the "A" range, as I enjoyed the material and felt confident. I could let my restless imagination run riot, so it seemed, and this encouraged me to delve into other areas, such as Philosophy.

I loved the arguments of Philosophy, the logical processes, and the apparent rigidity that I could fight against with my imagination. Time and time again I was told that I was a "flyer," but that I had yet to learn how to "walk," meaning, I had to learn the rules and expectations of Philosophical discussion, so I could present my ideas convincingly...I knew they were right, but even now I rail against the constraints of conformity. I tread a fine line between telling my own students to have a voice of their own, and advising them to follow the "rules."

It depends, I think, on what you are searching for. If you are at university solely because your parents are paying the fees and they insist you obtain a certain degree, then rules are important. It is conforming to the expectations of a standard education that will get you through, despite an absence of interest or delight. You *can* become an "A" student through sheer hard work and attention to detail, but my experience has been that most of these students are in the field of Commerce or Science - not the Humanities.

To obtain consistently high grades, "A's," in the fields of English, Art History, History, etc., something more is required (in most cases). The whole point about the Humanities is, after all, to teach us something of the human condition, of its strengths and weaknesses, its variety, its legacies and aspirations. These do not fall into the neat patterns of memorized equations, or tabulated data. By recognizing the symbolism in a picture, for instance, or a poem, one is led on a journey through many new and illuminating spheres: the historical context of the work (was there a war, a famine, an accident that inspired the work?), the personal concerns of the artist (Blake saw the mills of Europe as satanic, for instance). The more you investigate, the wider the scope of information becomes and the better equipped you become to deal with more sophisticated material. The requirement, for a First Class Humanities degree is a desire to understand, not just to "know."

Anyway, eventually I transferred up to U.B.C., and by then I had declared a major in Mediaeval Studies...only to change, at the last minute, to Religious Studies. I had done a bit of everything and had enjoyed the journey tremendously, obtaining "A" grades in all but two courses (B+ in Metaphysics - the course in which I was told not to "fly" too soon, and...you guessed it, my first Mediaeval Studies course!). I obtained my B.A., a "First," and went straight into the M.A. program, for which I received a full graduate fellowship. My M.A. was also a "First."

So, let's say you do have the inclination to aspire to greatness in your chosen field... what about some of the other factors that play a part in being a student? Choosing an education as an adult is a far different proposition to being placed in an institution as a child - especially if you are a mature student, like I was. There are many things to consider before you make the commitment, and even after you take the plunge, things will always crop up that will challenge you to reconsider.

Did you make the right decision? Is it all going to be worth it? For me, the moment of truth was when, only a few weeks before I was due to start classes, someone offered me a horse (the proverbial "gift horse!"), and another offered me a job I had been contemplating - a good job. What

2

to do? My lifelong dream had been to return to school, but I had also wanted my own horse again, and without the job I couldn't have afforded it. My decision was not an easy one, and there were times, when I was suffering "burnout," that I regretted not accepting the other path.

Now I have the experience of university behind me, of course, I know I made the right decision. I wouldn't have missed it for the world. Jobs end, pets die...a hard earned world of knowledge and understanding is with you forever, and it never stops growing.

Here are a few soul-searching questions you may want to ask yourself before you sell the house, quit the job at the bank, and revert to jeans and tee-shirts:

➢ Are you certain you are *ready* for University? Do you have young children at home - will this be a problem for quiet study, making classes, etc? If you are leaving high school, are you sure you don't want, or need, a break? Burnout is common - I experienced it between degrees.

➢ Are you aware of how you compare in ability to other students in your year/class? As a mature student, often you may be the oldest one in a class. Sometimes this is beneficial, as you can offer insight only life experience can offer, but some people can find it disillusioning (e.g., I was one of the oldest students in my Chemistry course, and I noticed how much quicker the younger ones were able to ingest the information...I began to feel insecure, which I think helped me decide to change my major). If you have misgivings about your background training, go to the resources office and ask for some old exams in the fields of interest, or do a preparatory course before you start the full term.

➢ Are you prepared to change your major if you find something more appealing? This is quite legitimate, honestly! I'm rather an extreme case, but, although most students are advised to declare their choice by the third year, there is no limit to how many times you can change it, nor how late you do it, as long as you show that you do, or can, meet the prerequisites (I caught up with those during the summer).

➢ How do you feel about increasing your knowledge in areas beyond the scope of your chosen career? Many students, I have to say, become blinkered. The first day of class, undoubtedly, someone will ask what will be on the exam...excuse me? What about learning something, what about everything in between?! The goal, the finished product - a neat degree under one's belt -

is not, as far as I am concerned, the most important thing. Yes, this guide is for the aspiring student, the one who wants to get "A's" - but it is intended, ideally, for those who wish to do their best, not just for those who want to impress. Doing one's best means expanding beyond the realms of immediate expectation and isolated goals. It means stretching the imagination, investigating, arguing, presenting things well, and pushing your own limits. Expand into new directions and learn!

➢ What kind of a student do you think you will be? Will self-discipline be a problem? Procrastinating is a curse of student life! It happens to us all, in the end, no matter how determined we are to maintain a tight schedule. One paper runs overtime, taking a few precious hours, or days, out of research time for another, etc. In the end, there is a mad dash to complete everything that is due, and some of the polish and spark you had at the beginning of term is lost to haste and panic! I've been there, too. I'll talk about dealing with assignments, later, but you need to be aware that this will be an issue, and decide early on how you will handle it. Consider how much time you can allot to: travel, scheduled classes, employment, study time (review), study time (preparation), home duties, special projects (research papers, etc.), social activities, sleep, etc., and adjust your expectations accordingly.

➢ Similarly, are you curious and keen to participate in class discussions, etc? Or will you be happy to just sit quietly and listen to everyone else? Some instructors push the participation aspect, while others are not too bothered - would you have a problem if you were called upon to contribute?

University is like every other project in life - if you take it on with a good attitude, with zest and enthusiasm, always attempting to achieve your personal best, then the outcome will be better than had you gone forward with trepidation or resentment - naturally. The thing is, though, the journey itself becomes a reason for trying - a goal in itself, and *that* is the joy of being at the peak of your abilities *and* under the influence of your fancies.

There *will* be times, I'll say again, when you wish you could pack the whole thing in - when an assignment becomes a chore and the "joy" I speak of is a distant flicker in someone *else's* eye. Although I love the learning process, and would stay a student for the rest of my life, given the choice, I am only half idealist. My alter ego is a realist, and I know that you will, as even I did, go through the doldrums. I can honestly say, though, that if you are doing well, and are truly interested in your work, the feeling will pass. Allow it to run it's course: don't listen to anyone's "helpful" suggestions to "cheer up" - keep reminding yourself that practically all the great artists, composers, and writers went through hell before they created masterpieces! Join the club and look forward to the creation!

Ignore, too, all the tired jokes about "student life" being one long party...if you are serious about excelling, it isn't. It is, however, one of the most challenging, exhilarating, and fulfilling experiences you can find in life, without jumping out of planes, or skiing down Everest! If you *want* to excel, the battle is half won!

If you are a Grade 12 student transferring straight into your first year at university without a break, I suppose, in most cases, you will not really have much of a choice in the matter, but the fact remains that this is still *your* life, *your* education, so you do have *some* control and *some* input. The best 'advice' I can offer is to make your first year as exciting and as enjoyable as you can. Be conscientious, though; choose courses that you know you will be interested in, with only one or two that may be more demanding. Pace yourself. Even if you are relying on a student loan or grant, that requires you to have a "full" course load, sometimes this can mean only five, rather than six courses. Take advantage of the spare time by applying yourself more diligently to the assignments in hand. If you over-stretch yourself in the first year, you will find keeping up with assignments – and therefore your grades – will be an effort that may not, in the end, pay off.

University is not the same as high school; you will be expected to have attained a degree of maturity, of worldly knowledge, of academic skills, and of independence. There will be moments when everything seems really strange and beyond you, but these are fleeting, and if you apply yourself with confidence, saying to yourself, "I've never had to do this before, but I'm going to find out how to do it, and I'm going to do it well," you will have taken that first step to being brilliant! This is your chance to immerse yourself a world of your *own* making!

(Just for your amusement, I have scattered a few "howlers" throughout the book - funny mistakes made by students on exam papers over the decades...like this one):

*"William the Conqueror was thrown from his horse
and wounded in the feudal system and died of it."*

CHAPTER 2: IMPROVING YOUR CHANCES

Having said all that, I know you are still concerned with how to obtain the best grades possible, and that is, after all, the main reason why I'm writing this book, right? So, without further adieu, let me share with you some of the tactics, procedures, stratagems, or what you will, that helped me climb to the top five percent of a large university (which is what I had to do to obtain my fellowship).

The Importance of Being Eclectic

I can't stress firmly enough the importance of an eclectic foundation. How can you be expected to challenge the philosophical issues in a novel, for instance, without understanding them *at all*? You can't be expected to analyze early Mediaeval works of art without knowing the tenets of belief which inspired them, nor can you be expected to appreciate the shift in artistic, religious, and philosophical themes/tone in the 20th century if you don't understand the impact of WWI.

I was in a third year seminar at U.B.C. one day, discussing various critical techniques in the study of comparative religions, when the subject of the War came up. I was stunned to find my comment, that the First World War was a watershed for many philosophical and religious beliefs, coldly received, even rejected with a titter by some of my younger classmates. Thanks to a quick-thinking instructor, however, the topic of the next session was amended to: "How War Affects the Train of Human Thought"! There was no tittering that week.

Everything, and I repeat, everything, is influenced by something else - the worst thing you can do for yourself is imagine that *your* chosen subject is the be all and end all. It isn't. Learn as much as you can about every subject you can. This foundation will stand you in good stead when you progress to higher study.

A true Renaissance thinker, which is what all aspiring students aim to be, is all-encompassing, embracing the sciences as well as the arts, so when there is an opportunity for you to watch a documentary on physics or astronomy (the show *@ Discovery* on the Discovery Channel is varied enough to suit everyone's tastes), or to flip through a glossy book about inventions, say, do so! In the long run everything comes together on at least one level - nothing is truly isolated.

If you are intent on improving your grades in courses such as English, History, Art History, Social Studies, etc., there is a general cross-section of knowledge that should be accumulated. Students today are, by and large, untrained in the field of philosophy and religion, yet these two subjects have influenced some of the most commonly studied works in literature, art, and even politics. It is not required that you have any sort of religious belief, yourself, nor that you can handle yourself in a debate - but an understanding of the various major belief systems, and a working knowledge of how to present a logical argument is essential if you are hoping to rise above mere "Average" in your studies.

Familiarization with mythological names and places; appreciation of the use of symbolism and allusion in both images and texts (see the appropriate sections in this book); recognition of influential historic events and people; a good command of the English language, with a varied vocabulary and better than average writing skills - this is what will make you shine.

Plan to set out on what I call a "fishing trip" to the library. Fishing trips are visits you make to a good, central library for the sole purpose of trying out new things. Go on a day when you have at least two or three hours to spare - time really does fly when you find something interesting! Go prepared with a pen and pad, some change for the photocopier (or buy a card if they sell them) and *an open mind.*

Begin by walking around the magazine / journals section: if anything catches your eye, have a flip through. I have found several useful publications that I never even knew existed, this way, as they weren't catalogued under the heading I had been searching under. Photocopy any articles you think may come in handy as reference material for courses you are intending to take. Creating one's own library of research material is something I shall mention again later, but for now, enjoy the freedom of investigating at your own leisure things you never thought you would! The more you enjoy the experience, the more information you will retain without even trying.

Move on to the stacks – don't go directly to the section you know already - go somewhere new. Maybe you are studying English Literature; don't go to the Literature section, but go, instead, to the History or Art sections. Just flip through the fun glossy books at first and enjoy the pictures. Get into the mood! When you find interesting items make a note under a suitable heading on an index card (see "Resources at Hand") for later reference (names of important books - and their call numbers - authors, journals, dates and details about historical events, particular art work).

On the way out, always take a moment to glance at the sale rack by the entrance - you never know what you may pick up for a dollar!

Music

In the 2000 UVSS (University of Victoria Students Society) handbook/calendar, I noticed, one of the notes on *How to Study* suggested that if you are trying to study with lots of noise around you, play some music on your personal stereo!!! Ahh!? Listening to music, research has found, is one of the most *complex* acts the brain can perform...why waste valuable brain power when you need it most? All you are doing is compounding the problem; besides, your ear will still pick up the low-frequency noise "outside" and you'll probably just end up with a headache. If you are bothered by noise, go somewhere quiet...the local library, a park - even your car!

Listening to music *before* you work, however, is often very good therapy for those who need to relax, or for those who need to sharpen their concentration. There is a popular theory at the moment which suggests that if you listen to Mozart's music for so many minutes a day you will increase your concentration levels...well...it doesn't actually have to be Mozart. The fact that he managed to write it at such a young age is inspiring - perhaps the theorists are suggesting that by listening to his music some of the genius of the man will rub off ? It's like consuming the god to become godlike! In actual fact, any decent classical music will have the same effect - all that is happening is that the brain is receiving continuous complex information. It is exercise for the grey-matter. Think of it as doing complex mathematics without equations - that is what music is, after all - an audible, mathematical language. Lofty stuff!

So go ahead, explore the wonderful world of classical music, even if you think you won't like it. There are many styles to choose from to suit your mood and taste, but be wary of these cheap "One Hundred Best Tunes" CD's because they are not conducive to relaxation or concentration. The whole point about listening to classical pieces to enhance your studying skills is to listen to something complex and, ideally, continuous. The brain automatically tunes in to a well-written work - it picks up on repetitions and themes, and recognizes when there is a lack of resolution. With most compilation CD's you will have pieces that have been edited to fit the time allowed - they end abruptly, or fade out just as you're beginning to enjoy them. There are some good collections out there, but you need to be selective. Borrow from the library, perhaps, until you acquire a taste for specific composers/styles.

If you really can't get into classical music, find something else - but not heavy metal, or "country" - choose something quiet and soothing, such as "Enya" or the various "Mood" tapes. Or try jazz - that works for some people, as the complexity can be on a par with classical music, yet the spontaneity and improvisation can make some, so I have been told, feel invigorated, ready to take on some serious study. Find something that is "you."

I truly believe music is a natural force, like sunshine - you don't need to play an instrument or read the black marks on the page to appreciate it. We are all born with an innate understanding of music - some of us exploit it and some of us don't. There is nothing to be intimidated by.

For those of you who are truly adventurous, try to become familiar with a few of the more famous Opera stories - if you really can't stand the thought of listening to two hours of Opera on your stereo, go to a live performance with a friend, or someone you know who likes this sort of entertainment. A good local production will give you the visual stimulation you really do need with Opera - after all, they were intended for the stage, not the CD! For the uninitiated I always recommend Mozart's *The Magic Flute*, as it is witty, lyrical and visually delightful. Otherwise, just read the libretto, the book of words. It will be a little like reading *Hamlet* straight off the page - rather flat and dry - but at least you will get an idea of the story line. There are a few Operas that are so often referred to that I can hardly imagine completing a four-year, top quality degree in the Humanities without bumping into at least one example along the way!

I recommend learning about Opera because it was such an important medium during the 18th & 19th centuries and has a bearing on many 20th century studies, such as its use as propaganda in WWII. Composers such as Puccini, Wagner, and Mozart (along with their respective librettists) wrote masterpieces which reflected contemporaneous events as well as mythological/religious beliefs. Being able to refer to such works with an efficiency only familiarity can fashion will truly earn you some extra "points."

Art

There are many artists and works of art of which the well-informed student should be aware. The potential list would be too lengthy to include in this type of manual. If you are planning to study anything in the visual arts or literature, it is wise to prepare yourself, beforehand, by ensuring you have a working knowledge of famous paintings, building styles and statues, etc. The student who can converse intelligently with the lecturer about "context" and "symbolism" is the student who will be noticed - if you are intent on rising to the top of your class, this is just want you want.

Whatever your major, I strongly recommend taking a course in Art History, perhaps as an elective, for you will see just how pervasive the information is (besides, the change in format, with slides, sometimes videos, etc., is a boon - an oasis - to any seriously industrious scholar). In modern films, even, it is sometimes the case that a director will incorporate an image, somehow, in his/her production, expecting the audience to be able to recognize it. Such a symbolic gesture usually appears in the form of a brief tableau, or in the echo of a few essential elements. If you can't recognize these, you may be missing intended "meaning." I've included a section on analyzing images, which will provide you with enough information to stay ahead of your classmates in any Art History class!

Again, use your library resources - browse, make a few notes, photocopy, etc. I would suggest making note of two or three major works from at least four or five artists from any given Period or School. For instance, choose two temples from ancient Greece, and three statues, perhaps. Move through the Ages until you reach an appropriate juncture, e.g., for students intending to focus on English Literature up to the Victorian era, end your search with the Pre-Raphaelites, perhaps. For those interested in subjects beyond this period, the focus shifts somewhat and your foundation will need to include Post-Impressionist and Modern art (as well as such things as Politics, Technology & Industry, Economics, modern Warfare, Environmental issues, etc., etc.).

Class Lectures

Let's begin with where you sit in class, as this says something about your attitude to learning. If you sit in the back row (by choice) you are usually considered disinterested, shy or indifferent. If you sit by the window you may tend to let your thoughts wander instead of concentrating on the lecture. Sitting immediately by the door tends to make you look like you can't wait to leave. This leaves the front row and the centre of the room.

If you are a confident person and like to show yourself as such, go ahead and sit in the front row, as near to the lecturer as possible - by the time you get to your third/fourth years in university you will find people vying for this position because, even if unconsciously, it still represents a certain status. If you are an independent thinker already, you should not have any reservations about showing the world you are proud of your educational goals. If you are still a little hesitant, sit somewhere in the middle of the room - away from distractions, but sitting squarely in the centre of the action. Move up one row per term, maybe.

Never be afraid to participate in the class discussion: there is nothing a teacher likes more than a student who is interested and involved. If you have to form groups, don't always wait for someone else to volunteer to take notes or be the spokesperson - *you* do it! However, be wary - there are students who will take advantage of your keenness, so every now and then surprise them by opting out, but make sure you still have your say.

Always make *your own* notes - if possible *before* class, e.g., when a reading has been assigned, or when you know that the instructor will be following the textbook closely, get ahead of the game - while everyone else is sitting with their heads down, scribbling every word into their notebooks, you will be relaxed and attentive. Every graduate or mature student will tell you that if you write something down you stand a much better chance of remembering it than if you merely photocopy it, or read someone else's notes. Relying solely on class handouts is not wise, and your papers/assignments will, ultimately, show your restricted initiative.

If you like to bring a tape recorder to class, remember that this format is only as useful as you make it! You *must* play the tapes again and again, while you are driving, washing dishes, etc., to reap the benefit (and remember, this shouldn't really be an *alternative* to note-taking).

Note-taking is a skill that is acquired through practise. You may not become proficient until well into your second or third year, so don't worry if the process is a slow one – you're in good company. Just be aware that you are trying to "cut down" and if your hand is aching at the end of a class, realize that you are probably writing too much!

Class notes, as reading notes, should only reflect material you *need to learn/study*. This may sound simplistic, but think about it. If you are studying *King Lear*, for instance, do you really need to write down the fact that he has three daughters, or the fact that Edmund and Edgar are the sons of Gloucester, just because the instructor mentions these details? Of course not, but many first-year students will do just that, thinking that the instructor's word is paramount. Soon, their notebooks are jammed with almost every detail, and by the end of the term they have all but rewritten the play! Then comes the task of filtering out the notes that *are* relevant: the "stuff" that will be on the exam (e.g., you know full well that you won't be asked: "How many daughters did Lear have?").

The trick is to limit note-taking to the bare essentials, e.g., key words, basic thematic concepts, comparison & contrast suggestions. Do a mind-map (see diagram in the section entitled, "The English Assignment"). Always anticipate the exam, writing in the margins any potential exam questions and then highlighting the specific details relating to them - especially when an instructor shows particular interest, or jokingly says "I'll be putting this on the exam": nine times out of ten it *isn't* a joke!

A word about instructors. Not meaning to sound revolutionary, I must say that I do encourage my students to be opinionated, to challenge, and to request further information, especially if something seems wanting. As a "for instance," I had a young student who was taking an English course with an instructor I had heard about through the grapevine; this instructor seemed, so everyone concurred, to have a problem allowing her pupils room for interpretation.

She "told" the class what a poem meant, and she dictated how a novel was to be understood, leaving no chance for individualism or imagination. I heard, later, from a mature student in her class, that she admitted to this tactic because it was easier and quicker to mark the assignments. How sad. This, thankfully, is a rare case, and in my own experience instructors relish someone brave enough to take the pressure off *them* for a few minutes!

Don't be a "know all," or disturb the flow of the lecture too regularly, but do, *do*, *do* have your say. Remember that you are paying for this formal education, one way or another, and that the instructor is there to provide you with the assignments, background information, and a helping hand if needed. It is *your* learning process, *your* journey - seize it! Remember, though, it may be wise to acknowledge the teacher's slant, preference, etc., especially when preparing for an exam! It's a bit of a concession to the "system," but it's one that will benefit you in the end.

Formats

There are always alternatives to any given method of study – don't be afraid to experiment and branch out a bit on your own. For example, you are given a weekend assignment to read Shakespeare's *Hamlet* and write a one-page essay on the prince's reaction to his mother's remarriage. Well, you can either read the play from the flat page and hope that you fully grasp all the subtle nuances, etc., or hire a version of the play on video.

A few years ago there was little to choose from - Hollywood black & white versions were too clichéd, the BBC productions were stiff and boring, and even the more recent Mel Gibson attempt left something (or rather a lot) to be desired! In such productions you would have gained the impression, for instance, that Hamlet was either "somewhat peeved" with his mother or was suffering under an Oedipus Complex, etc.

Now, however, we have the brilliant and exciting Kenneth Branagh production! All four hours are riveting. Indulge yourself! (Shakespeare's plays were *intended* to be appreciated in a visual, not literary medium). In this well acted and visually stunning performance you can actually feel what Hamlet feels - you can almost touch the anger and disgust...and Gertrude's fear of (and for) her son.

Be discerning, as you investigate these other formats - never forget to follow the original in your book, as many versions done for the screen (especially older ones) have great swaths of material missing. Any enactment of a written word, I believe, however, offers you a chance to see at least one other interpretation, besides your own - and this is essential.

If a particular version of the video has been recommended, and you deviate from this, choosing another on which to base your arguments of interpretation, first discuss it with your instructor - accept others' expertise, but make a few decisions of your own and show that you are mature enough in your skills to defend them. If you can put forward a sound reason for choosing one option over another, you not only show initiative, but you may even convince the instructor to amend the suggestion for the rest of the class - that is a feather in your cap! (One of the references I opted to send U.B.C. when I applied, was from a teacher who found my input "impressive" enough to mention.)

Study Area

In order to be an efficient student you must have a decent place to study, and this is doubly important for those with family at home. Relying on the kitchen table, a cushion on your lap in front of the television, or your bed, really isn't the best idea. Sometimes these places will do, for reading, making quick notes, etc., but for serious work you need a good desk. I tend to spread out while I'm working, and I like to keep everything as close to hand as possible, so I have a six-foot table as a desk! Even this I can cover with "fall out" quicker than you can say "Jack Robinson!" It's so handy, though; there is room for my computer at one end, books along the back and space for papers and pens and all that important "stuff" one tends to accumulate while researching.

Have the table/desk up against a wall, not overlooking a window, or too near a door as distractions are anathema to the serious student. On the wall facing you have a large pin-board for notes, articles, a calendar, etc. Add a few inspirational quotations (printed out) and *read* them from time to time. Frame a swimming certificate, a spelling award, anything that makes you think of learning and success. The positive attitude you create about you in this study space really does make a difference to your thinking processes.

Add a little something which reminds you of your dreams and aspirations, to make you remember to strive just that little bit harder: I used to have a picture of the Rover on Mars on my wall and a model of the Space Shuttle on my monitor (well, I said "dreams," didn't I?), but now I have a bust of Michelangelo's *David*. What does that say about me?!

As your academic sophistication increases, your tastes and influences change, so adapt your working area to suit. I tend to have a massive clear out just before I really get stuck into a new project - all the pictures come off the wall, everything unnecessary is shifted to the storage area, and then I have just a bare room, except for computer and books. It's a grand feeling, and clears my mind like nothing else can!

As studying can get quite serious, it's a good idea to have a break every now and then and drift off into a daydream...they are very therapeutic, you know, and can be as effective in replenishing your brain as a catnap.

When possible, keep a nearby window open slightly, even in the cooler months, as fresh air helps you maintain your attention and actually speeds up the cognitive processes.

Chapter 3: Being Resourceful

The student who is limited to the textbook, and a few books in the university library when a research project is due, is not an aspiring student. It is vital that you expand your horizons. There are ways of doing this that are cheap, if that is a concern, and non-invasive (into your regular school work) if that is an issue. First, I want to mention some of the things you can have in your own work-space, which should set you up for any Humanities course; then, I want to suggest a few other avenues of study you may want to consider.

Resources at Hand

Post-It Notes! How did we get through the centuries without them? I find the small 1" size the best because they have room for one thought, one page reference, etc. When I was writing my Master's Thesis my desk looked like a flock of Monarch butterflies had landed on it! If you don't like highlighting in your text books use these to mark important pages - use key words that will remind you why you marked it.

Index cards are just as indispensable to the diligent student. Keep an indexed file-box handy and jot down notes all the time, wherever you go, whatever you watch. When you are reading, or talking with classmates, keep a record of all those snippets of information that you may, one day, find useful. File them alphabetically, according to the main theme, or word. I did this for my Thesis research and thank goodness I did - so many gems, from obscure quotations to translations, to bibliographic references came spilling forth from this continually growing source. If you have a specific project on the go, keep a separate file for this, concentrating solely on the subject in hand.

There are a few reference books that any good Arts/Humanities student should possess:

Two Dictionaries: One should be fairly modern, to include recent scientific terms, new words, etc., but I strongly recommend a good old-fashioned one as well, especially if you are taking English courses. The dictionaries compiled before, say, 1950 have words in them which modern editors have deemed defunct but are commonly found in older literature. Usually, they have the English spelling option which is useful for those who resent the American spell-check on the computer. Before you click those buttons to "replace" what you thought was a correct spelling, check the dictionary version. The older dictionaries are easy to find in places like Value-Village where they will range from $1.99-$5.99. A really good one will have additional mines of information like lists of foreign phrases (great for impressing the instructor), familiar allusions, or mythological names.

A Bible: Don't get the King James Version unless you find you need it for specific quotations, etc. A good, plain, English text is much easier to read and understand. In fact, for the purpose of getting to know the biblical stories as background knowledge for symbolic interpretation and allusions, any book that tells the major stories for children will suffice (and remember, Part Three of this book, "Gods Galore!" is intended for this purpose). You really do need to have a basic understanding of the Judeo-Christian tradition for many of the topics in the Arts/Humanities, especially if you are focusing on the western tradition. Obviously, if your interests run in a more easterly direction, make sure you are familiar with the story of the Buddha, the Hindu epics, etc. (Don't rely on a Bible Dictionary because many of these presume a certain degree of knowledge about the subject and you can't always be sure how much of the information it offers is superfluous to your needs). The more you can learn about the early Church, too, the more you will understand certain allusions to the "Fathers" and the Crusades.

A Thesaurus: The computer version is not adequate - it may be handy, but a good paperback copy will give you so many more choices.

A History Time-line Book: These are great for checking up on authors and their works, historical contexts, wars, paintings, social influences, religion, science.

A Concise Dictionary of Philosophical Terms: This doesn't have to be grand, just a Penguin paperback will suffice. Often authors presume their readers are acquainted with terms like *a priori* and *a posteriori* - don't just skip over them and hope for the best - take the time to look them up and be determined to know what they mean the next time you encounter them...undoubtedly, you will!

A Book of Quotations: For adding that special touch to a paper or essay, or for finding out the name behind a quotation an author expects you to know, a resource for quotations is priceless and inspirational.

> *I hate to hunt down a tired metaphor.*
> **(Byron)**

The MLA Handbook: Formally called The MLA Handbook for Writers of Research Papers, this is a MUST for all University students, as it demonstrates the most widely accepted formats of footnotes, endnotes, bibliographies, etc.

The (Canadian/American) Writer's Handbook: More extensive than the MLA Handbook is this catalogue of information - it shows you **how** to write a good research paper, essay, etc., and offers tips on grammar, syntax, compositional styles and much more. For anyone who has the least difficulty with writing formal papers, this is indispensable.

An Atlas of the World: Make it a habit to check the location of the place you are studying!

Miscellaneous: Obviously, stock up on books that you anticipate will be useful to you in your chosen field of specialization. If you will be focusing on Classical Studies, gather around you anything you can find on mythology, art & architecture, Roman rulers, Greek philosophy. If your penchant runs to English Literature such as Milton, find out what was influential to his work and get some background information, e.g., on the Calvin movement, or metaphysics. Whatever your major, try to accumulate as many books on essay/research preparation as possible - the MLA Handbook is a good start, but there are specialized texts that focus on Literature, History and the Sciences, and so on.

Old textbooks are useful, especially those written before, say, the 1940's, because they tend to be a bit more formal and full of detail than modern texts - many have pictures, charts, etc., that you may be able to reproduce in your paper with the knowledge that no one else will have the same thing (make sure the facts haven't changed since the book was written, though!). Art History books are always a great investment, especially if you have a scanner at home.

17

You don't need to go to any great lengths to build a decent library for yourself - go to second-hand stores (especially Value-Village), garage sales and flea-markets. You can find wonderful books for a song! When you are on a roll, snug in your study area, the last thing you want to do is go out to the public library, so why not keep your own? If you are working on a major paper and are using several resources, go ahead and photocopy essays from Journals, etc. Keep them stapled together and file them properly when you get home. These then form part of your personal library and can be perused at your leisure. By the time I had completed my Master's Thesis I had enough photocopied material to fill two blue recycling boxes! (**N.B.** Be aware of the Photocopying Laws, as posted near the copying machines).

You need not worry too much about having up-to-the-minute research at your fingertips - new books are ridiculously expensive and unless you are writing a Master's Thesis, or perhaps an Honour's Thesis, they simply aren't worth the expenditure. Besides, authors who publish scholarly books usually have segments of their work published in journals or periodicals (some authors actually make revisions of their published works, or clarify certain details the book versions didn't), so it is to these you should refer for the bulk of your material.

If you require monographs (texts written on one subject usually by a single author) try out alternative libraries - the average student will tend to take whatever is handiest, but you (the aspiring student!) should seek out special collections, other university libraries (interlibrary loaning). If you know early on in your university career that you are going to concentrate on a particular topic, it's worth getting an Associate Library Card from these other places - it may cost you, but if you are seriously intending to excel in your field the sooner you make contacts and check out the resources, the better for you in the long run.

Make use of the library orientation tours that are always offered at the beginning of term, or make an appointment to have a librarian take you through the use of the CD-ROM Index, the Stacks, the Research Indices, Microfiche machines, etc. You'll need to know where to go to get the information you want (I have more to say on this in the "Research" section).

Other Resources

Besides books and articles as resource material, what about the Internet, Television, Video and Audio recordings, Museums and Lectures? Anyone, or all of these can offer something to the discerning student. Be wary, though.

Although many documentaries are stimulating and colourful to watch, they often make what are called "blanket statements," statements which are too generalized to be taken seriously - they certainly shouldn't be quoted. T.V. documentaries are for general audiences who really only have a passing interest in Egyptian tombs, or Shakespeare's England. They are good, however, for those students who wish to steep themselves in a particular subject. If the show is done well, you may come away with a greater appreciation of your topic, perhaps even a few ideas for further research. That is what learning is truly all about. You can memorize names and dates, but it is the synthesis of knowledge, interest, appreciation, and curiosity that makes the ideal independent thinker!

The Internet is useful for finding indices of books and articles, and for having short documents e-mailed to you, etc. Be aware, though that many older works may not have been listed on the Web (unless you find a site specifically geared toward these), and many up-to-the-minute papers found in academic journals may only be available in hard copy for several months after publication. Check out the information sheets in the university library and see for yourself how useful the on-line system will be for *your* level of research. I have more to say on this subject, too (see "Research").

Video & Audio recordings are worthy of your attention, especially if you are majoring in English. The best recordings of Shakespeare's plays/poetry are from the British studios, with British actors - the lilt and the nuances of the English (British) voice are perfectly suited to the job and tend to keep the listener more attuned to what is being said than many American versions seem to (after all, the language of Shakespeare's day would never have been heard with an American accent!). That is a personal preference, perhaps, but see (or rather, hear) for yourself. Don't be afraid to pause and reflect on what is being said - make notes and discuss.

Museums and public lectures offer the student so many riches, if exploited correctly. I understand the difficulty with some museums - they can be static and uninspiring. If you don't enjoy going to museums, but you are willing to give it another go, ask ahead of time for personal attention (if available). Tell the docent (the person who usually wanders around answering questions) what your interest is, and that you are researching for a paper. Be as efficient and as polite as you can and you never know, they may let you into rooms not usually open to the public, or allow you access to drawers normally locked.

From personal experience, I find that the sterility of museums which house every single artefact behind glass, is disturbing - I feel so much more involved and interested if there are things to touch. If you are given any opportunity to hold an object, enjoy it, as this is the best way to feel a connection with your chosen topic (and this can include texts, textiles, pottery, tools).

As for Lectures - keep an eye out for the free lectures sponsored by the university, or keep in touch with organizations in your field which may invite guest speakers, etc. Don't think that your classroom lectures are all there is - after all, you are being exposed to only one or two perspectives - allow yourself the opportunity of getting alternative 'angles' on a subject.

Check out the bulletin board outside the main office in the department you are interested in, as there are always posters there pertaining to relevant conferences and lectures. When you go to these, take pen and paper, make notes, be brave and ask questions, talk to other people (including the guest speakers, afterward) - get yourself known as an industrious student. (It helps to read up on a subject before hand, too!)

The serious student may also consider enrolling in an extracurricular Continuing Education course related to his/her major, or even just for interest. Many of these are quite affordable and offer the potential for a new perspective and extra resource material. It may be the case that your regular classes are all you can handle, time-wise, but the CE courses seldom, if ever, require you to do homework - just think about enjoying the lectures, seeing slide shows and getting the handouts.

There are even groups of like-minded individuals in the community who meet informally to discuss particular topics - they come from all walks of life, some scholarly, some not. At the University of Victoria such groups fall under the heading of SAGE (Stimulate, Advance, and Guide Education). You can either join a pre-existing group, or you can form your own. Most universities will have a similar program - check it out. Likewise, specialized centres on campus that cater specifically to your field of interest are worth joining, even as a non-contributing (off-campus) member. The newsletters, free lectures, and independent library resources will be worth the nominal membership fee.

There is also the correspondence course route - work on something really interesting in your own time - increase your expertise. Although it would be more beneficial to you to receive the tuition with such courses, you can opt out of this and pay only for the course-work. You can audit a course. This way you receive all the texts, handouts, videos, or whatever, and read them just for your own enlightenment. If you choose to accept tuition, you also have the choice of applying your final letter grade to your degree, or not: remember that *credits* are transferred, not grades, so even if you didn't do as well as hoped, the credit earned may free you up for another interesting course later!

The industrious, outreaching student is the one who will write interesting papers, argue informatively, and be confident that alternative resources have been referenced. I recall helping a student do some research for a Philosophy of Science paper: the topic was the acceptance of robots into society. We came across two descriptions of an experiment involving a robot that were utterly contradictory (in two separate sources)! Which one was right? Rather than being side-tracked by another branch of research, we decided to use this discrepancy *within* the argument of the paper, to quite good effect, actually. Had we not deviated from the "suggested" reading list, we would never have come across this, and the uniqueness of that particular argument would have been lost...the paper received a high "A."

Employing a Tutor

I would like to mention a few things about tutors, as I am one, myself. There are still some misconceptions out there regarding people who hire tutors: I had one mature gentleman who kept our visits a secret until he heard that another of his classmates was also coming to see me! Others seem to think that I am here to do the work *for* them, to write their papers, even, and I have had more than one offer of "big money" to do this. Needless to say, I rejected them all.

Tutoring is a service that is intended to help a student *understand*, be at an assignment, a text, or a procedure. It can take the form of a private but formal lecture (I even had a blackboard at one stage, but now I live in an apartment, I don't have the room), an informal question/answer period, or a practise session on writing essays, etc. Tutoring is not "proof-reading," or "editing."

There are countless advertisements on the university notice boards for students offering their services as proof-readers/editors, and this is fine...so long as they are getting the kinds of grades you are aiming for! Be aware that each person has a unique writing style, a standard of proficiency, that may or may not be suited to your needs. One person, for instance, might skim over your work, find nothing blatantly in error, point out a few spelling mistakes, and charge you $20. Another, given the same paper, may notice weakness in your argument and offer a suggestion - or find something not quite right about your set up - she will write comments in the margins, make several corrections, all to make it possible for *you* to then go back and rewrite a good, sound paper...again, for $20. The onus is upon *you* to take this advice and use it.

Finding a suitable tutor is like finding a good doctor...take your time. There is nothing wrong with shopping around, but give each person a few attempts before rejecting them. If something is amiss, or you are uncertain of his/her tactics, ask for a free consultation and discuss the matter. Any tutor worth his salt will oblige. Some of the qualities I, knowing what I know now, would look for, are:

✓ **maturity:** someone older, naturally, has more experience (both academic and "life"), and it is this experience you are most going to benefit from.

✓ **patience:** if a tutor, like many doctors I have met, seems to watch the clock, constantly figuring out how much time is left in the session, or gets impatient with you when you can't grasp an explanation, perhaps this one is not for you.

✓ **a good grade record:** obviously, you don't want someone who regularly got "C's" in university advising you. Ask what her record was like.

✓ **a willingness to listen as well as talk:** this, I have found out for myself, comes with experience.

✓ **interest and expertise:** if a tutor has no interest in a topic, it shows. I sometimes get Commerce students coming to me to proofread papers in that subject. Because this service is different, impersonal even, my total lack of interest in business affairs is irrelevant. When people come for tutoring, however, they come because they know I specialize in certain subjects within the Humanities, and so my interest (and, indeed, expertise) is always evident. Some tutors advertise assistance in two, three, even four very different fields (such as one in the local paper recently, offering help in History, Physics, Geography, and French), and I find this a bit disconcerting. Yes, this person is obviously a "Renaissance thinker," and I admire him for that, but few people (other than the da Vincis of this world) can master so many spheres and then go on to relay that mastery to others successfully...at university level.

Once you have discovered someone with whom you can work, stick to him/her. Get to know him. Ask about his life as a student, what made him choose their field, and tutoring, etc.

Offer some personal information about yourself. This is a partnership, remember. Two minds working together inevitably learn about each other, but speeding up the process never hurt.

Always try to be punctual. That is one of my pet peeves - tardiness. If you have made an appointment, keep it, or phone with an explanation. Politeness doesn't cost, and your relationship with your tutor will be strengthened by these little details!

Know what help you are expecting. Arriving with the play *Othello* in your hand and saying "I don't know where to begin," is not the best way to introduce yourself. Read the play, *try* to answer the questions, prepare *some* sort of outline for the assignment. Make a list of the questions *you* want to ask, or, if you prefer, make an appointment for each Act of the play: ask that you just sit and discuss each Act and make notes as you go. That way, you have all the information you require to complete a rough draft of a paper without overdoing it, and you can ask questions when you think of them.

Listen to advice, take in all the suggestions, correct errors, but, and I shall say this time and again, in the end the work has to be yours...not the tutor's. Accept that a few things may get lost in the translation, that your way of phrasing an idea may not, in the final draft, sound as it did during your session. You may think of something better, you may not. You may get an "A," you may not. Your chances, though, of improving, or maintaining, your overall standing are vastly increased with the aid of a good tutor.

I say "maintaining," because I want to offer you another personal anecdote: when I was taking first year Philosophy courses, I received "A's" on all my papers...but when I went up to second year classes, the first paper I handed in - to the same instructor I might add - received a "B+." When I asked why, he simply said: "You're in second year now, and you're still thinking like a first year." He was being extra hard on me because I had expressed an interest in pursuing this field as a major and he took me under his wing just a little, I think. I took on some out of class tuition, with him, and learned how to develop my argumentation skills. I ended up maintaining my overall "A" standing.

Think about this: a good tutor is normally not required beyond the first year, certainly not beyond the second.

"The appendix is a part of a book for which nobody ever found a use."

Chapter 4: Assignment Time!

So, you have been given an assignment. You begin thinking about achieving that important high grade, and this edge is good, but try not to lose sight of the bigger picture - the learning process itself. How you approach the job, and what techniques you employ will get you half way there before you actually start writing.

Let's take a simple English assignment, as an example, and work through it together.

You will get nothing written or created unless Minerva helps.
(Horace)

The English Assignment

Begin each assignment the day you receive it - not tomorrow, not next Wednesday. The moment you set about it, you have made the task easier for yourself to finish.

How do you begin? Many students think that they must conjure up a title first, and they sit there, for an age, trying to imagine a catchy phrase. A title, rather, will often be the very least of your concerns, and can really only reflect the content of the paper once that paper has been written, right? The first, thing, then, is just to sit and go over the wording of the assignment. What, precisely, are you asked to do? Again, a common mistake is to think you know what is expected, write a full paper in one sitting, hand it in, and get a "C" because you strayed too far from the question in hand.

Example

Read this short story:

BIG BANG

The hour hand was missing. Not that it made much difference out here in the middle of nowhere.

"Anybody know what time it is?" queried Seth, squinting into the merciless rays of the sun, pretending he remembered how to tell the time by the pattern they made through the clouds...or something.

"For Pete's sake man, throw that thing away – it's twenty past seven," shouted the team leader over his shoulder without turning to look at the last member of the expedition, who was tripping over just about everything in his temporary semi-blinded state.

"Look!" Three voices were heard in unison, and three arms stretched out toward the horizon toward a little group of derelict shacks, huddled around a long since abandoned white-washed church.

The last one to arrive, stepping through a low doorway, Seth entered a cool and darkened room. The smell of rotting wood and the distinct odour of animals hit him like a clenched fist and he fanned the air in front of his face for several minutes. All around he saw the sorry remnants of life; everything had been reclaimed by nature, as if the occupants had been chased away and warned not to look back.

From the flickers of daylight which penetrated this desolate place through the cracks in the ceiling and the broken doorway, was illuminated an object, a small silvery sphere, down on the floor. Brushing away the cobwebs and the scurrying roaches with his foot as best he could, Seth bent over, balancing on one foot, and swung his hand down to raise his find. Expecting it to be relatively heavy, the man with the broken watch misjudged the physics of his movements and, in finding the object too light as to offer any resistance, fell headlong into a carpet of beetles and broken wood. Smacking the creatures from his trouser-legs and shaking his hair (just in case) he uttered a few profanities and tried again.

Looking rather worse for wear than he had when he had gone inside, Seth exited the little home with the exciting new object tucked carefully under his arm.

"Hey!" he called, hoping to impress the rest of the team who had, so far, considered him to be a bit of a fool, a bit of a liability. Noticing the reflection of the sphere as it caught the sun's uninterrupted rays, everyone showed a keen interest to examine it.

"Reckon it's worth anything?" One asked, his mind already calculating his share in the profit.

"Were there any others?"

"Be careful with it, it may be dangerous," warned another.

Just as this last word of wisdom came, Seth felt the dreaded tickling of a moving creature beneath his shirt. It was beginning to make that clicking noise he hated so. It was a beetle.

"Ooohh!" came the forlorn moan of a man in utter agony and frustration. Instinctively jostling to rid himself of this unwanted visitor, Seth's grip on the sphere was lost and it tumbled to the ground.

On impact, the little silver object shattered and from it shot a thousand pieces, flying out in all directions. Some were too bright even to look at, some were spinning, some changed shape, and a few turned black and seemed to have some sort of magnetic effect on the fragments nearby. It was a strange sight indeed.

Looking at Seth with an air of disbelief, the team leader scooped up one fragment of the shattered sphere. He raised it up to the light, his head shaking and one eye still on the dishevelled Seth. There, on the outer surface of the fragment was what seemed to be writing...English! Hurriedly the group gathered up the remainder of the sphere, placing the shards together. With three large segments placed side by side, the sphere revealed its secret. There, inscribed in small print, scratched but readable, were the following words:

"Fragile! Please find enclosed, as requested, all required materials for CREATION: BUILD YOUR OWN UNIVERSE. Guaranteed to give hours of enjoyment. For added excitement, invest in our latest upgrade, LIFE SIGNS: THE WONDERS OF CARBON."

The End...Or is it the Beginning?

This is your assignment: **Discuss Seth's role in this story, with reference to the deeper philosophical themes implied by the concept of the "Big Bang."**

(Although some guides still insist on the basic six questions: *How? When? Where? Who? Why? What?* which are perfectly legitimate and a great place to start, these are a little simplistic for someone aspiring to top grades.)

First of all, you need to recognize two things: the "deeper philosophical themes," and the meaning of "Big Bang." The latter is fairly well known, but some people may not be acquainted with the scientific *theory*, i.e., that the universe, simply put, was created from a massive, single explosion of ultra-dense matter. The philosophical inferences in the story include the major question: Where did we come from? Also, though, are the more subtle, metaphysical allusions to Time, the god concept, and the quest for knowledge.

Next, you want to create a mind map - a casual, freehand chart of your ideas, something like this:

This map will help you organize your thoughts about, and reactions to, the story. Don't worry how messy it gets, as long as you can follow your own train of thought - no one else has to see this. The idea is to get you making connections, asking questions. Why, if Seth is such a klutz, does *he* discover the object, and not the expedition leader, for instance? Is it because he is destined to drop it, to break it, just as he trips over things and breaks his own watch? Is this foreshadowing?

It is ironic, then, that such a misfit should become analogous to a god, creating a whole new universe, but then, you must ask whether our universe is just a mistake, or perhaps a finely tuned mechanical machine that is run by an impersonal computer program. Why is the writing on the object in English? This implies that whoever created the object was familiar with Earth languages...but such advanced technology is out of place - anachronistic...so how do you explain it? Get the idea?

All the time, you want to keep Seth in mind, as he is the focus of your assignment. Everything you think of, ask yourself how it affects your understanding of his character. His role, then, in relation to these concepts, becomes one of catalyst, perhaps instigator, even creator. His is an ironic situation, for he is in a group of knowledge-seeking individuals, who remain at a distance, while he, stumbling blindly, discovers the secrets of the universe! What does this say about our scientific quest?

The mind map is an organic entity - it grows with your familiarity and understanding of the work in hand. Keep it visible at all times while you are working, and add to it, or detract from it as you wish.

Next, you need to consider how long a paper is expected. Let's say 1000 words, which, typed (double-spaced) on the computer, works out at approximately 250 -300 words per page, give or take a few. That means an essay about four pages. Don't try any tricks with point size or margins – they've all been done before and it really isn't going to impress an instructor if he knows you've gone to all that trouble to get out of a few more words. Besides, if you are intending to better yourself as a student, you don't want to fall into bad habits, right?

So, four or five pages are needed - do you find that daunting, or restrictive? Until you have "proven" yourself to your instructors, stick within the guidelines; once you have acquired confidence, style and control, expand your horizons a bit and discuss with the instructor the possibility of writing a longer paper. Sometimes the added responsibility boosts the ego and earns you a better grade just for the bravado!

A 1000 word essay will contain about seven or eight decent paragraphs, including your Thesis and Conclusion. The next step is to create an outline for these:

1.   Thesis: Seth is an unlikely godlike character who instigates the creation of a new universe.
         His character and actions work to emphasize profound philosophical ideas.
         E.g., concepts of Time, godliness, knowledge.

2. Seth asks what the time is, introducing one of the main concepts.

    His watch is broken

    Time therefore relative - introduces idea of Time as a universal (Einstein?)

    Time is recreated when he breaks the sphere (new universe)

    Is this the end or the beginning, or both?

3. He is a klutz, yet he discovers the object.

    Concepts of fate, responsibility, etc?

    Falls over it: thinks it will be heavy...concept of ignorance, danger, opening Pandora's Box (e.g., science)?

4. Ironic that he, rather than the expedition, finds the object.

    Quest for knowledge not always an easy path/predictable.

    Would this constitute a scientific advancement - could it be replicated? What would be the controls? Science a series of lucky accidents?

5. Through his actions, Seth forces the reader to question the possibility of other civilizations, other dimensions.

    The writing is in English - why?

    Possibility that it is our own civilization, but in the "future"?

    Are we alone? Time travel, etc.

6. Accidentally becomes godlike.

    Challenges religious beliefs?

    Has the opportunity to create Life, too.

    Reflections of Frankenstein?

7. Conclusion: Seth's role is one of catalyst, possibly creator.

    He is a misfit, a klutz, yet he manages to create a universe, albeit inadvertently.

    His actions invite the reader to deal with complex philosophical ideas about the origins and nature of the universe.

Now all you have to do is fill in the missing sentences that link all these ideas together! It's simple, really – it's finding the ideas that's the main effort, here. Notice how some points are left as questions: this allows me to remember my train of thought without lingering too long on the outline - I can expand on the details in the text itself. Also, note the similarity between paragraph 1 and 7, the Thesis Statement and the Conclusion. Although you need to write a basic T.S. and Conclusion for this outline, remember that this is just a working draft - you can change anything in it as you write.

Thesis Statements (and Conclusions)

A thesis statement should contain two essential elements: the topic of the paper and your argument, opinion, etc. It should always appear as near to the beginning of the paper as possible, preferably in the first paragraph, for a paper of this length, though longer papers have the flexibility to be adjusted somewhat. You should always keep it in mind as you prepare your final draft, making sure you have fully supported your statement and have kept to the issue in hand.

The general gist of your thesis statement should also appear in your Conclusion, worded slightly differently to avoid mechanical repetition. By referring directly to your thesis statement at the end of your paper you are saying, in effect: "This was what I said I was going to do, and this was how I did it!"

A good introductory paragraph also tells the reader how you intend to present your point of view. Here's an example of an introductory paragraph for the assignment on "Big Bang":

Seth is an unlikely godlike character who instigates the creation of a new universe through careless actions. By analyzing the sequence of events leading up to the "Big Bang," in light of Seth's clumsiness and ignorance, it will be shown that his character and actions work to emphasize profound philosophical ideas, such as when Time begins or ends, what constitutes godliness, whether there is a "correct" path to knowledge, and whether there are other dimensions to this universe, or, indeed, other universes.

Your Conclusion, then, reiterates this in other, more specific terms, incorporating some of your major points as evidence that you succeeded in doing what you set out to do. As such, the Conclusion is bound to change somewhat from your original outline, for while you write, your ideas take shape, details are stressed or downgraded.

Some general tips for writing up the assignment:

- Avoid repetition, generalities and excessive wordiness.

- Be concise, use details, examples and references to support your statements.

- Be aware of continuity in your writing - do the sentences and paragraphs link well with prior and subsequent sentences/paragraphs?

- Never be afraid of expressing your own personality in your writing - use words you like, ideas you want to defend, but be careful not to stray from the assignment, or to use biased or loaded language!

- Get someone else to proofread your work...I always miss my own mistakes!

- Revision/editing of a composition is *vital*: two, three or even four drafts is not uncommon.

- Make it a habit to read your essay out loud - most mistakes reveal themselves.

This, then, is how you approach the average English assignment. Poetry can be a bit trickier, so I'll mention that when I discuss symbolism and allusion (below). I won't go into details about the technicalities of writing - this isn't that type of guide, besides, you should get acquainted with the MLA Handbook and other Style Sheets.

Being Analytical & Critical

One of the most important qualities of the above-average student is the ability to be analytical, objective, critical. By the time you get into your third year you will (hopefully) have an idea of what you will be majoring in - your classes will be getting more concentrated and more will be expected of you. You will attend seminar classes, which means that you will have to do some research, some presentation, some critiquing of others' works, etc. You need to refine your analytical skills before then so you can be ahead of the game.

Being analytical and critical means that you *question* whatever it is you are told to read/watch/research, etc. Cross-examine it as if it were a person in court! If it posits a theory make sure that it offers enough evidence to support it - is the evidence solid, hypothetical, erroneous? (If there are mistakes in grammar, sentence structure, etc., make note, if it helps your case, but don't be too picky). Is the argument logical? Is it propagandistic, racist, outdated? Is there a lot of superfluous material - perhaps there is not enough material? Are there references to issues or facts which don't ring true, or aren't convincing? Research them - find out why.

Other questions you may ask, depending on the nature of the material being critiqued, include:

- Is the document, article, etc., written by someone of authority or experience?

- Is the thesis clear and fully supported?

- What is the perspective of the author?

- Are the data manipulated to serve an ulterior motive (e.g., statistics)?

- Does the work offer any unique contribution to the field, or is it merely a rehash of other people's ideas?

- What is the weakest aspect of the work?

- The strongest?

In the case of a *critique* assignment, you are expected to be objective: you point out the weak and the strong, the good the bad and the ugly! One of the first critique jobs is to critically analyze another student's paper (usually a report on a story, play, or poem), so you need to maintain your distance - forget who wrote it and focus on what it says. Have they grasped the major themes? Did they understand the symbolism? Why didn't they mention something *you* think is important? (If you know something is erroneous, suggest an *alternative* way in which the student might have presented his/her material, so as to emphasize the correct information without simply stating that they were "wrong").

Critiquing other people's work forces you to take a good look at your own understanding of the assignment – it's a great tool the instructor is giving you...use it well! Usually such critiques in class are only returned to the students if they ask to see them - *do so*, and learn from what others have said about *your* work. In time you can even critique the critiques, for many students simply attack the paper they are given, pointing out all the errors in spelling and style, whilst omitting to acknowledge the well-written parts and, more important, failing to challenge erroneous statements. Such practises separate the average from the aspiring students.

Symbolism & Allusion in Literature

There are three main categories of symbolism in literature:

Contextual / Circumstantial

Contextual: An author or artist develops a symbolic pattern that is independent of any external, familiar symbolic pattern. For instance, an inanimate object may take on special meaning in the story because of some persistent thought or action of one of the characters.

Circumstantial: The significance of an object, etc., can change with time and/or perspective, e.g., the swastika, which was once an almost international symbol of peace and prosperity, but now has darker connotations since the rise of Nazism.

Cultural

Symbols used within a specific culture, or used to represent a culture, e.g., flags, coins, anthems, mascots, etc.

Transcendental

Platonic in concept, these symbols are intended to represent something beyond, but linked to, the human experience. E.g., religious symbols, the eagle (a common symbol of power throughout the world), an hourglass, or a ticking clock to depict Time, etc. These are most commonly the "universal" symbols, recognized by most people, whatever the language.

In "Big Bang," both contextual and transcendental symbolism is used. I'll let you ponder on that one.

Allusion, on the other hand is a subtle, or obvious, indication of intended meaning or reference. This is what is used most often in poetry, I find. It presupposes knowledge of certain traditions or themes and is often harder to work with than symbolism because of this. Arthur Miller, for example, alludes to famous paintings in the staging of his plays, but unless you are very familiar with a great deal of artwork, or you had been in on the creative process, how could you possibly know *which* paintings, or why?

You cannot learn *how* to recognize allusion...you just do. This is where all the extra learning comes in handy, all those hours browsing in the library, watching documentaries, listening to operas. The more you are exposed to, the more you can distinguish!

When dealing with a poem, though, your best bet is to keep a good dictionary near and look things up. A good dictionary of myths, fables, sayings, etc., is an excellent investment. So often a poet will mention names from ancient Greek tales; perhaps he will allude to another poet's work, in which case your book of quotations will be useful, so you can discover who it is. Analyzing a poem fully can be a lengthy process, involving several avenues of investigation.

"A boy who looks at the future before it arrives can then look at the past."

Exercise

Locate a copy of W. B. Yeats' poem, "The Second Coming"...

Here are some of the things you should know, or investigate, in order to fully comprehend this intriguing work:

- What is the "Second Coming"? Usually it pertains to the Christian belief that Jesus would return to Earth after a period of tribulation.

- What is Yeats' background? (1865-1939); began his career as a romantic poet; studied existentialism of Nietzche and became involved in the Irish Nationalist movement; disillusioned with the results of the revolution and the rise of the Irish middle class; withdrew from society to a country house in order to write "serious" poetry; style changed, and his work became symbolic and metaphysical, exploring questions of identity and history.

- If you don't know the word *gyre*, look it up.

- What would the falconer straying too far from the falconer to hear his voice symbolize, in terms of religion?

- "...the centre cannot hold" and "...anarchy is loosed upon the world..." tell of what kind of social difficulties. How would this relate to Christianity?

- What is the "blood-dimmed tide?" This poem was written in 1920-1: what major events had taken place to which this phrase may allude?

- What is the "ceremony of innocence?" What about innocence itself...why the "ceremony"?

- The word "revelation" is used as allusion here: revelation is the sudden exposure, etc., of "an unknown" - yet the term is linked to the Second Coming - a "known" (but awaited) phenomenon within the Christian tradition...this is done in order to allude to the Book of Revelation - the New Testament account of Jesus' triumphant "return." It is an ironic usage.

- Look up *Spiritus Mundi*.

- What does the creature sound like? What does it remind you of? (Hint: Egypt).

- What link is there between Egypt and the Christian faith?

- Note how the beast moves - what is suggested here? (Hint: think of the use of "thighs" rather than "legs," for instance...and...)

- What other event took place at Bethlehem?

- What was "asleep" for twenty centuries, then troubled by a rocking cradle (i.e., the birth of Jesus)?

- What is it that is going to be born?

It would also help you to know that in another work, called *A Vision*, Yeats describes his idea that history evolves in two-thousand year cycles: the birth of Jesus had ended the Greco-Roman period, and the cycle was about to end with the fall of Christianity and the rise of a new paganism - a polytheism. So, the "Second Coming" turns out to be that of paganism, not Jesus!

This is a standard first year poem assignment...I have done it several times with students. If you can answer all these questions, prepare your paper as suggested, and fill in the missing links smoothly and convincingly, you will almost certainly earn yourself an "A" grade.

So, generally speaking, setting about analyzing a literary work for symbolism and/or allusion means that you are going to be asking things like:

❖ Do I know anything about the author's background? When was he writing? What were his beliefs? Did he have an ulterior motive for writing this, such as a political position to defend, or a religious dogma to support/refute? (E.g., some authors were known to be social satirists, certain poets were caught up in revolutionary causes, etc.)

❖ Is the work *itself* political, historical, religious, fantastical? What is the overall theme?

❖ Does the title offer any "clues" to help my overall interpretation? Be careful, here: often a title is the last thing on the author/poet's mind and often it is a partial quotation from another work that alludes to some general concept, or it is purely symbolic or even purposefully misleading (e.g., Yeats' poem "The Second Coming").

❖ How would I describe the overall tone of the work? Is it positive, negative, passionate, satirical, sombre?

❖ Is there a multi-layered story going on? Are these layers connected in a purely functional way, e.g., to link characters who might otherwise not interact? Or, are they symbolically reflective of each other?

❖ Are there any nouns that have been capitalized to make them proper names? Why would this be done? (Answer: to imply, usually, that the work is an allegory, telling one story under the guise of another, like *Gulliver's Travels*, or *Candide*).

❖ What about the names themselves - could they be symbolic? Could a name have been used as a subtle allusion to someone/something else?

❖ I've underlined everything I think is meaningful:

> figurative language
>
> references to religious, historical or mythological figures
>
> unusual objects, places or actions
>
> detailed descriptions of places, clothes, faces
>
> repetition
>
> reflection / introspection

❖ Does each element tally with my overall impression of the work, or are there elements I simply can't make "fit"? Maybe I have the "wrong end of the stick"? (If you find that 25% or more of the material you thought to be meaningful doesn't support your overall interpretation, perhaps it is time to rethink the matter.)

❖ What do I do now? Even if you find that your interpretation "works" first time, go back and *read the work again.* (Note: if the work is long, and you haven't the time to do a complete reread, just skim-read; if it is a play, watch a production of it on video, etc.) Knowing what you think you know *now*, about its "meaning," do you have a different reaction to it? Does everything flow easier, or have you unearthed even more questions to ask?

Just as a little extra information, it is good if you can recognize the three types of imagery in literature, which sometimes go hand-in-hand with allusion and/or symbolism, but are certainly part of your overall analysis:

Literal

This imagery presents the audience with clear image of something physical. An example would be: "The grass in the field blew in the wind." Simple, literal.

Depending on the context, this wind could be symbolic.

Perceptual

A bit more complex, perceptual imagery incorporates figurative language, such as similes and metaphors. Expanding on the grass theme, we would have: "The grass in the field blew in the wind like a storm-tossed sea." Again, the story in question may have a recurrent "sea" theme, or this image may suggest trouble brewing, etc.

Conceptual

Here we have my favourite, for it opens up and plays on the imagination by incorporating scenes that cannot occur naturally. "The grass in the field blew in the wind like a storm-tossed sea, as Mrs. Murphy sipped the concoction Joseph had slipped into her glass and there, in an instant, she lifted from the ground and began to float away." You can have fun with this one! Is the wind an intentional precursor to the magic? Is it the wind or the potion that sends Mrs. Murphy flying?

CHAPTER 5: BASIC RESEARCH

Research consists, mainly, of three tasks:

1. **locating** source material, usually through various indices
2. **reading** swiftly and accurately
3. **writing** concise and accurate notes

The Library & the Web

I don't want to get too involved with the basics of library usage, as you can go to any library and discover this for yourself - you should certainly try to exploit the orientation classes at the university before you have an assignment...in fact, most first years are given one class in the library. You will be given a few exercises to perform, such as...

1. Which card catalogue system is used?
2. Can you take periodicals out of the library?
3. Where would you find the latest information on solar energy?
4. List three books by Aldus Huxley
5. When were they published?
6. List three magazines/periodicals which regularly contain book reviews.
7. What are the library's hours?
8. Are there photocopy machines on every floor?
9. On which floor is the Microform department?
10. Is there Internet access?

...and you will be taken around and shown where everything is, but I, personally, don't think this is enough. If you want to do good research, you need good skills, and these must be acquired through practise. I think you will learn more, and retain the information, if you take the time to perform the real functions of research on your own, taking all the time you need.

The key to researching at the "A" grade level is to venture beyond the realm of investigation most students deem adequate for an assignment. For example, the average first year student, especially one transferring directly from high school, will almost always head for the Internet, or the general subject heading in the Stacks (the main area of the library containing books, rather than periodicals, etc.). From my own experience, the latter is more useful than the former.

"William the Conqueror landed in 1066 A.D. ...A.D. means 'After Dark'" ???

Despite the popularity of the World Wide Web, I still believe it is not used to its potential efficiency, as far as undergraduate research is concerned. Part of the fault lies in the material itself: recently, I had cause to read some articles gathered from the Web by a student of mine. She was studying a video artist and had given me everything she could muster...what I received were a few short biographies, a lengthy but uninspiring interview transcript, and a few *atrociously* written commentaries. There was enough material to write the two-page outline she had been assigned, but had she been attempting anything more sophisticated or challenging, she would have been at a loss.

You have to be discerning: you cannot write a top quality paper using inferior sources. If you are going to cite electronic sources, do so with care. This is not my area of expertise, so I won't go into detail about it, but I can recommend a great book on the subject of online citations (and, surprisingly, there are few of them about): *The Columbia Guide to Online Style* by Janice. R. Walker and Todd Taylor (New York: Columbia UP, 1998). There is also *The Learning Highway* (Trevor Owen, et al, Toronto: Key Porter, 1995), which guides you through the various methods of accessing and exploiting the Internet for research.

Needless to say, though, there are a few basic, common sense caveats:

✔ Never rely on general web sites as your main sources - although you can legitimately cite these in your paper, at higher levels of research you need sources that can be verified, and much on the Internet is tentative, to say the least. Even those sites which can offer factual information are usually very generalized, for mass, cross-section audiences.

✔ If you are developing a major paper, or an Honour's Thesis, for example, where your bibliography becomes an inherent part of the project, and on which you will be judged to some extent, I would suggest you limit your electronic sources to academic databases and online periodical articles that have been uploaded from hard copy.

✓ This doesn't mean you cannot be inventive and imaginative, and use a variety of items, ranging from e-mails to videos, to chat-room messages, but know in advance that these will only provide diversions from monotony: seldom will they be given much credence by the upper academic echelons, as they are too insubstantial, and (it is a shame perhaps) have proven unreliable in terms of validity and precision.

✓ Always provide as much information as possible when citing an electronic source: remember that it is still the work and the author you are making reference to, not the site itself. This is a common error I see almost every day, as I proofread papers. A student will have in the footnote: *www.world'send.ca* ...this tells me next to nothing. I need to know:

> (a) the name(s) of the author(s)
> (b) the title of the article that the information came from
> (c) the date it was published on the Web, or, if unavailable, the date you accessed it
> (d) the place of publication and the publishing house (it may be an Internet address)
> (e) the *full* address of the site (URL)

As far as using the library is concerned, rather than heading straight for your own little corner of the Stacks (which I am not discouraging, as I have often simply browsed through the books in the search for inspiration, images, quotations), go, instead, to the Research area and learn how to *use* the Indices (usually, the orientation librarian will only have time to point these out to you, not take you through the steps of using them - and they do take some getting used to). There are simple guides to subject headings, and more complex guides to articles, authors, citations, that can start your search off with a sense of organization and direction.

For the more popular magazines (e.g., *Scientific American*, *Time*, etc.), try the *Readers' Guide to Periodical Literature*. This is how the (latter) entries will appear (boxed numbers for your reference only):

[1] BEETHOVEN, the poet

    [2] Ludwig, the Man Who Wrote Musical Poetry. [3] J. Tyson [4] bibl. [5] il.

    [6] Journal of the Deaf Poets Society [7] 187: [8] 159-61 [9] Ja 21   01

[10] TYSON, Janet

    Ludwig, the Man Who Wrote Musical Poetry. Il. Journal of the Deaf Poets Society 187: 159-61 Ja 21 '01

[1] Subject	[6] Name of magazine
[2] Article title	[7] Volume # :
[3] Author(s)	[8] Pages
[4] Bibliography	[9] Date of magazine
[5] Illustrated	[10] Listing under Author.

The *Humanities Index*, on the other hand, has a broader subject category and deals mostly with the chief scholarly journals, not books or popular magazines, etc. This is where you will want to spend your time is you are delving deeper into any topic.

For those of you who really want to get into the thick of things, I've included an exercise I give my own students. The resources you will need are listed, but, of course, if your university has slightly different versions (e.g., publishing dates), etc., the information may be slightly amended. I set this exercise up in 2001, so not much will have changed, I think, other than a few more citations. Try it, and see what you think: the answers are provided (cover them up!), so you can check your progress. This will be the very groundwork of much of your research, so it's best to do it often until you speed up the process. Choose a subject at random and try again.

For the legend in any of these texts, always check the inside of the front cover - if you need to keep reminding yourself which column of information is which, or what abbreviations mean what, photocopy that page and keep it on top, where you can constantly refer to it without returning to the front of the text each time.

You will need:

Library of Congress Subject Headings (22ⁿᵈ ed.)

Arts & Humanities Citation Indices, 1985: *Permuterm Subject Index* (LITE to Z)

Citation Index (A to LEE)

Source Index (A to KOCK) 3.

Exercise

1) From the *Library of Congress Subject Headings*, state the number of subdivisions listed under Rome - Foreign Relations. _____

2) You are studying Constantine I:

    1.   What are the years of his reign? _____

    2.   What is the topic listed after NT? _____

    3.   Of which subject heading is this entry a sub-division? _____

    4.   Of which heading is it a second sub-division? _____

3) From the three volumes of the **Humanities Index**, locate the following information:

    Find the **subject** heading *Rome-Pagan*. How many authors are listed under this heading? _____

    Which of these two authors has used the word "Rome" in their article title?

    _____

4) Locate WHC Frend's entry in the *Citation Index*.

    i.   In how many articles is Frend cited? _____

    ii.   How many different publications do these citations appear in? _____

    iii.   How many of these are book reviews? _____

    iv.   What years do the publications span? _____

5) In the *Source Index:*

a) How many entries appear under Frend WHC? _____

b) The article *"The Rise of Christianity"* is in a 1985 source:

        1.   It was originally published when? _____

        2.   It appears in which 1985 journal/periodical? _____

        3.   It covers how many pages? _____

        4.   It appears in which volume number? _____

        5.   It uses how many references? _____

Answers

1.   **6**

2.   1. **306-337,** 2. **Saxa Rubra, Battle of, 312** 3. **History**   4. **Rome**

3.   **2**   **Both** (+ sign indicates)

4.   i.   **18**

       ii.   **12**

       iii. **6**

       iv. **1983-85**

5.   a). **6**

       b) 1.   **1974**

            2.   **AM Scholar**

            3.   **5**

            4.   **54**

            5.   **4**

Reading for Research

What kind of reader are you? I don't suppose you have ever been asked this before, but reading style and skills can make quite a difference to the time and effort spent in doing research.

Moving your lips when you read, for instance, can slow you down a great deal. Different jobs require different reading rates, so if you read everything at the same speed, you may be limiting your efficiency. Going over a line several times, or regressing, is time-consuming and unnecessary in most cases where research rather than analysis is required: learn how to glean information from context (e.g., when there are words you do not recognize or understand).

Reading for research is not the same as reading for pleasure, or even for an English assignment. Literally, you need to learn how to "skim" over the surface of a written page as quickly and as carefully as you can, picking up on main ideas, recognizing significant passages, and being able to eliminate everything that is of no use to you. It is a skill that requires practise, but in time, one that will *save* you time as well as effort.

When you have found a potential source, the first step to take is the overview:

➤ Open the chosen book to the Table of Contents. If each chapter is sub-divided, choose a sub-title which you think may be of interest to you. If these don't appear in the Table of Contents, flip through the chapter itself and make a mental note of the sub-headings.

➤ When you have an overview of the chapter in question, go back to the beginning and skim-read just the first two or three paragraphs. You should find the main idea of the chapter and the bias, or argument of the author.

➤ Go to the end of the chapter and read the last few paragraphs, where you should find a closing statement which acts as a summary or conclusion. If the chapter contains material you want to use, go back to the body of the text and skim-read.

These are the basic "rules" for skim-reading:

✓ Look for changes in the *type* used: *Italics*, **boldface**, larger print, underlining, CAPITALS, etc., all indicate emphasis of one kind or another and should be noted.

✓ Look for question marks, exclamation marks, diagrams, maps, charts, etc.

✓ Look for phrases such as "The argument here is..." or "The contention is..." or "Therefore, we submit that..." or "In conclusion..." or "To summarize," etc.

✓ Don't feel that you have to read every single word. Meaning can be gleaned from key words.

✓ Practise reading entire phrases simultaneously, rather than one word at a time.

✓ If you locate a passage you wish to *use* but find an individual sentence proves difficult, break it down, slowly, into its subordinate clauses. Research reading is, by its very nature, an overview activity, but if you are employing material as a reference in your work you need to understand precisely what is being said and how to use that information effectively.

Exercise

Cover the second paragraph and read the first one:

...success...this line of treatment...depends...great extent...good growth of horn. Cod liver oil...great help...this respect, but if...growth... very slow...stimulant applied...coronet is useful also. In long-standing cases...hoof section...performed with advantage. By giving almost immediate relief...pressure within, hoof section can...quick...dramatic results.

Now read the second one:

The success of this line of treatment depends to a great extent upon good growth of horn. Cod liver oil is of great help in this respect, but if the growth is very slow a stimulant applied to the coronet is useful also. In long-standing cases, hoof section may be performed with advantage. By giving almost immediate relief to pressure within, hoof section can give quick and dramatic results.

With practise, your eye will pass over words like "the," "is," "and," etc., and you will increase your reading speed while retaining comprehension. The highlighted words are those that should really become unnecessary also, with practise. The final sentence contains only one piece of information you haven't seen already – "...immediate relief to pressure."

This kind of reading is recommended only for research purposes and *first* readings of literature - remember that when you have an assignment to *analyze* a work, you must read it several times over, becoming progressively precise in your attention to detail.

When you have completed your overview and skimming of a text, the next step is to go back to passages that you think you will use and pick out the main idea. This isn't always as easy as it sounds, as many paragraphs have three or four sentences which could be mistaken as the central theme by a careless or too hasty reader. Practise with a few paragraphs from a book you have not read before - skim read them, one at a time, jot down what you think was the main idea of the paragraph, reread it slowly and see if you were right. Did you miss something the first time?

Exercise

Find, from a non-fiction text, as quickly and as accurately as possible, the following information:

Title: _____

Author: _____

Publisher: _____

Copyright Date: _____

Edition Number: _____

Library of Congress Catalogue Card Number: _____

Does it contain illustrations? _____

Is there a Preface? _____

What does it say its purpose is (summarize in one or two sentences)?

_____

_____

_____

Is there a bibliography? _____

How many chapters are there? _____

Can you see any sub-headings within the chapters? _____

What section would you say constitutes the Conclusion (sub-heading title)?

_____

Skim over the final paragraph - what *is* the conclusion?

_____

_____

Are footnotes or endnotes used? Which? _____

"Homer was not written by Homer, but by another man of that name."

Taking Notes

When you are researching, not only do you need to be able to read quickly, you also need to be able to write notes quickly and efficiently.

Keeping an index-card filing system for your own notes is the best and most common method of note-taking/keeping. The usual 3" X 5" size are most convenient, and these should be kept in a proper box with an alphabetical index. When you have completed your skim-reading and overview steps and you are sure you want to use a particular text as a source, proceed to jot down on your cards the following information:

- The full title of the text
- Its call number
- The author, editor or translator
- The publisher, city and date if it is a book
- The journal, volume/issue date, and page numbers if it is an article
- The main idea of the passage you are interested in, with page number in parentheses

- Any (short) quotation you want to use, with page number in parentheses
- The number of any footnote you want to use
- In the upper corner of the card write one or two key words under which will give you a quick idea of its contents later
- If you run on to two or more cards clip them together

Obviously, you can write your own thoughts on these cards, too, such as your opinion of the work, or ideas that have come to you as you have read, but *do not* try to paraphrase lengthy passages. You will invariably end up with something erroneous. Put your own thoughts in parentheses, or in a different colour pen - better yet, simply put the page number down, with a key word to mark the paragraph and use the card simply as a reminder to go back to that particular resource and read it properly when you need it.

You can file cards under the last name of the author, or under a general subject heading, depending on how complicated your project becomes. Some students prefer to keep a bibliographical index separately - with another file for notes. It's up to you. Personally, I find a separate bibliography file is great, as you can just take the cards out of the box and type up your Bibliography without searching all over the place again.

Try not to fit too many notes on one card - you should have one or two concise (and related) ideas with the supporting information. Think of them as brainstorming tools - you should be able to throw them all on a table and play with them until you get a pattern that makes sense, or inspires you (more on this when I talk about revision and exams). Keep every note you make until your paper is handed in and out of your control!

When you have collected useful information for your project, you must begin a thorough scrutiny and analysis of the work. You must be aware of the impact a quotation, or excerpt, or reference will have on your work as a whole. For a top quality paper, you want to be certain that the material you use is suited to your purpose - by this I mean that anything you cite should, even on closer scrutiny, support your intentions in using it. Some students flip through a few books, find some neat sounding quotations and simply insert them into the body of their paper without really thinking about context.

Remember, though, that in most first year courses anyway, the assignments have been established for some time, and the resources are probably well known to the instructors, so if an author is cited out of context, or is misquoted, it *will* be noticed. Imagine your paper is a newspaper article written after an interview with that author...you asked him a very important question, then didn't bother to listen to his whole reply, and just picked out the bits you thought might impress your readers. The next day, you receive a notice of liable: the author is taking you to court! If the overall *original intention* of the chosen passage clashes with *your* argument, decide whether to use it, or to leave it and find another quotation.

Ask yourself such questions as:

♦ Can I introduce this material in a coherent and consistent manner?

♦ Have I made note of the author's bias, if any, and allowed for possible contradictions?

♦ If the work does clash with my thesis argument, can I still use it to help argue my case? (Don't be afraid of offering up one or two objections to your own work, but supply adequate rebuttals - use your research to back up your own idea, or the idea of someone you are arguing for, etc. The more you can prove that you have thought of "everything," and that you can graciously acknowledge other opinions, the better your grade will be than if you simply stand on a soapbox and declare only *your* view.)

♦ Does it contain words, allusions, events, etc., with which I am unfamiliar?

♦ Have I sought explanation of these?

♦ Am I simply including this so I can add the source to my bibliography and thus "pad" it out?

♦ Have I used the most recent version of the work?

♦ Has the author changed his/her opinions, findings, etc., in a subsequent version? Should I mention this in my paper?

♦ Have I read any reviews of this work? How was it received? Should I use critics' arguments?

The more familiar you are with the information you are working with, the better your paper will be. The more you can question, compare, argue, support, the better your grade will be, almost certainly.

When you are at the stage of reading selected reference material *thoroughly*, keep a good dictionary to hand and *use it*! Understand what you are reading! A College Dictionary can be one of the best resources you can have.

"Bacon was the man who thought he wrote Shakespeare."

Primary & Secondary Sources

One of the simplest aspects of a good research paper, especially once you have progressed to more advanced projects, is the classification of sources. I had heard of "primary" and "secondary sources" before university, but had never realized what, exactly, the terms signified. I used to think they simply designated more important sources from less important ones...hmmmm.

Example

You are writing an essay on the Roman/Jewish War of 70 C.E. The following is a breakdown of possible primary & secondary sources:

Primary	Secondary
Dead Sea Scrolls	*The Last Battle*, H.G. Holly
New Testament	*Masada and the Martyrs*, P.N. Gill
Josephus (*Wars*)	*Josephus and the Wars of the Jews*, Harry Box
Heroditus	*The Roman Influence in Judea*, G.N. Leighton

Can you see the pattern? Primary sources are usually related to your topic in a direct way - they were written in the same period and place, or they were written as second-hand accounts soon afterward. They offer information which has not been re-written by a third party, or broken down and employed to support someone else's thesis. If you are studying Victorian poetry, for instance, any original poem you refer to in your analysis becomes a primary source. Use your own discretion - if in doubt, ask.

Secondary sources, then, are the rest of the sources you use, such as articles, books, essays, video clips, newspaper articles, etc. Generally speaking, a secondary source is material which has been written *about* the topic *you* are wring about. It is the result of someone else's research.

A good, well rounded, major paper should have separate headings in the bibliography for Primary & Secondary Sources. For smaller papers the segregation of sources is not always necessary, but it's a good idea to start as you mean to go on, and if your instructor queries why you are being so formal, tell him/her that you are intending to progress to bigger and better things and little details like this need to become second nature to you!

Exercise

Identify primary sources with an asterisk and secondary sources with a circle **and** put the entries into correct order (again, the answers are on the subsequent page - cover them before you begin):

Culpepper, R.A. "The Johannine HYPODEIGMA: A Reading of John 13." **Semeia** 53 (1991) 133-152.

The Other Bible: Ancient Alternative Scriptures, W. Barnstone, Ed., (New York: Harper, 1984).

Penchansky, David. "Staying the Night: Intertextuality in Genesis and Judges." In *Reading Between Texts: Intertextuality and the Hebrew Bible*. Louisville: Westminster, 1992. 77-88.

Hill, John Spencer. " 'ta baia ton phoinikon' (John 12:13): Pleonasm or Prolepsis?" **JBL** 101.1 (March, 1982) 133-135.

Steinmetz, Devora. "Vineyard, Farm and Garden: The Drunkenness of Noah in the Context of Primal History." **JBL** 113.2 (Summer 1994) 193-207.

Omanson, R.L. "What's in a Name?" **BT** 40.1 (January, 1989) 109-119.

Josephus. *Josephus: Complete Works*, Trans. W. Whiston. (Michigan: Kregel, 1960).

Greek-English Lexicon of the New Testament and Other Early Christian Literature, W.F. Arndt and
F.W. Gingrich, Eds., 2nd ed. (Chicago: U of Chicago P, 1979)

" 'Habeas Corpus' was a phrase of the Great Plague and means 'Bring out your dead'. "

Answers

* = Primary   O = Secondary   (**Semeia**, **JBL**, and **BT** are journals)

1. Culpepper   **O**
2. *Greek-English Lexicon of the New Testament and Other Early Christian Literature*   * **O**
      (Primary or secondary depending on use. Can be placed under "Acknowledgments")
3. Hill   **O**
4. Josephus   *
5. Omanson   **O**
6. *The Other Bible: Ancient Alternative Scriptures*   *
7. Penchansky   **O**
8. Steinmetz   **O**

As you have guessed, no doubt, these texts come from my own research. Number 2, the
Greek-English Lexicon, is a reference work that is normally cited in the "Acknowledgements" of a
major work, along with other dictionaries, encyclopaedias, etc. It can be a primary source because
it deals with language, or a secondary source because it will, by nature, imply certain subjective
interpretations of language. Categorizing it depends on your usage (as an undergraduate, though,
you probably won't have to worry too much about this sort of thing, unless, of course, you are keen
to display your advanced skills!). Also, as with number 6, the *Lexicon* has at least one editor, so
unless you are citing something he/she has written, directly, you must site the text itself, that is why
the title of the book is used for alphabetizing. Josephus, number 4, is listed under his name because
the work is his, but in translation.

General Tips

Just to wrap up, then, here are some various tips on the creation of your research paper (and take a look at the essay in the "Philosophy" section of this book):

✓ Always try to include the latest information on your topic - usually found in the Periodicals & Journals section. Monographs (works written on one specific topic, usually by one author) are preferable, but some collective works are just as useful. Avoid "survey"- type books.

✓ It really looks like you have done your homework if you can refer to well established works in the field - the people and writings every other author seems to be familiar with.

✓ Always be aware that authors have a personal bias - it is inevitable. Check the biography of the author (if there is one) or read the preface to see the "slant" in any given text. Argue against it or use it to your benefit.

✓ If you are concentrating on only one or two scholars' work, research the sources he/she has employed - if you want to argue a point, you must know what you are talking about.

✓ Look through the bibliographies of current articles to get ideas for other places to search.

✓ Always check both the card and the computer catalogues.

✓ Check out *other* library offerings - not all periodicals in one field, for example, are held at general libraries, so you may need to investigate other, more specialized libraries and arrange a visit or an inter-library loan.

✓ *Never* use any quotation, information, etc., without providing reference details.

✓ Don't photocopy *everything* unless you are really pushed for time. When I was doing my M.A. Thesis, I was living on Vancouver Island and commuting to U.B.C. at regular intervals. The specialist library on campus was the only place I could obtain certain materials, but I usually had to catch a ferry the same day, so I was pushed for time. This was how I acquired such a vast amount of photocopied material. Most of it was useful, because I did my skim-reading, but a few were not. Allow yourself time to skim-read in the library - you will end up with more relevant material and more change in your pocket!

✓ Always refer to your Handbook for specifications on presentation of footnotes, endnotes, bibliographies, etc. Forcing yourself to do it correctly the first time will save you hassle later on and will help your work look mature and professional.

✓ All your careful research will not pay off unless you pay attention to your writing skills. Mistakes in tenses, spelling, format, etc., will reveal a lack of concentration that will not be conducive to high grades.

✓ *All* papers require more than one draft. Get it proofread, if possible.

✓ Keep an index-card file of useful books, authors, journals, references, quotations, etc. File them alphabetically or by subject.

Chapter 6: Analyzing Visual Images

Many of you will be taking at least one course that deals with images, rather than words, be it an art history course, or something in the field of architectural, or mediaeval studies, perhaps. Applying yourself to the analysis of symbolism will skyrocket you to the attention of the instructor and the higher grades you are seeking.

When analyzing any visual works, you want to be asking questions such as:

❑ In which medium is the work? E.g., Wood, stone, cave painting, fresco, oils, etc.

❑ Does the medium help in any way to convey meaning? For instance, if a sculptor has the skills and the choice of working in stone or wood, and he chooses wood, is there something he is trying to express by emphasizing the "living" medium, the lighter, softer medium? (Be careful, though – don't presume there is some ulterior purpose in using wood...it may just be that the tools and the skills were not available for anything more sophisticated.)

❑ Is the painting done in oils because it is a strong, vibrant, flexible medium, or because the artist was fulfilling his formal training by *experimenting* with oils - does he revert to another medium later in his career? (A similar question may be asked of any medium if there are alternatives available.)

❑ Does the image adhere to any particular genre? E.g., Iconography, Impressionism, Flemish still life, portraiture, etc.

❑ Is this the genre for which the artist is best known?

❑ Do I know enough about the artist to make any comment on his/her "style"?

❑ In what period was the work created? Was this period highlighted by significant events such as wars, revolutions, famines, discoveries, etc?

- If the work is classified as "Ancient" or "Prehistoric," or even "Tribal," were there any natural phenomena that might have influenced the design - e.g., a local river-system, a cliff used for killing prey, a mountain with sacred meaning?

- What were the religious/philosophical beliefs, if any, of the people/artist concerned?

- Is the subject material obviously linked to the period, or obviously disassociated? For instance, if War is the central theme, does the war being depicted "match" the period in which it is set? Perhaps the war is mythological, allegorical, or purposefully anachronistic?

- *Deviations from period require explanation.*

- This applies to dress, too. Is an historical character dressed in a style that reflects the period of the painting, rather than his/her own period? Can this be explained by artistic "trends" or is there some other reason?

- Is the work complete? If not, why not? Was this the last work before the artist died? Was he interrupted by some event? Was the work intentionally left unfinished to express some subtle meaning or make some "statement"?

- What could be symbolic in the image? E.g., Look at the main objects in the foreground of the painting, or at the front of a sculpture - is there an unusual arrangement of objects? Is there someone standing in an awkward, or "attention grabbing" manner? Is there an interesting use of colour, clothing style, facial expression, etc? Are there any animals in the image?

- Is there an architectural element to the image, implied or obvious? How could this be significant? Does the style reflect a certain ideology?

- What could be allusion? E.g., Do I recognize any mythological or religious references?

❑ Is there something in the image that looks out of place - something I can't relate directly to the main subject? Can this be reconciled to my research?

❑ Have I given a uniform interpretation to all the symbolic elements in the picture?

❑ Does each detail "fit" my overall explanation of what the painting "means"?

❑ I have found several elements that do not correspond to my overall impression, what do I do? (If you find that 25%, or more, of your in-depth analysis [e.g., you have found *several* small details in the painting - legible writing on a piece of paper, a bowl of fruit that has been disturbed, a fly on a window, etc.], or any one of the *major* aspects of your interpretation [e.g. you think a painting is making a comment on the French Revolution, but the image is of a small child picking flowers in a field...] fails to firmly support your idea, you should consider rethinking the whole approach.)

Example

For this introduction to image analysis, you will require a large, clear, colour copy of the famous painting: **The Marriage of Giovani Arnolfini and Giovanna Cenami**, by Jan van Eyck (Flemish) 1434. Any library with a section on fine art should have it.

This is some of the background information you should know, which, again, is readily available:

▪ The title was attributed later, by scholars. It bears no title of its own.

▪ Flemish painters were the first to use oils instead of fresco (colours tempered with egg yolk). It was this new medium that allowed for the famous Flemish detail and colour! Van Eyck perfected the technique.

- Eyck was primarily a portrait painter.

- He was sent by the Duke of Burgundy on confidential missions into Spain & Portugal.

- He was described as having a "biological passion" for homeliness, embellishing wrinkles and blemishes. He scrutinized the faces of his subjects with a keen eye and was fascinated by their psychological secrets.

Now, to the painting: the following are details that have been discovered through superficial research, and ideas for their interpretation:

- The painting's subjects are a cloth merchant from Lucca (Italy), and a banker's daughter.

- There is no written record of this marriage. Although this was not particularly unusual for the times, in the case of lower class individuals, it does suggest the possibility of secrecy, for this couple is well-to-do.

- Given the nobility/political connections of the painter, the couple may be friends of Duke.

- The setting for the marriage is a bedroom not a church.

- Weddings at this time in Europe were sometimes held in homes.

- Traditionally, the man went to the woman's house to collect her for the marriage ceremony, then took her to his own house. In this case, the ceremony takes place in the woman's home, it seems.

- Blessing ceremonies were usually performed in the doorway of church - the door of the home is reflected in the mirror.

- In the 15th C a marriage could simply be a legal agreement with 2 witnesses, with no priest present...

- ...but this was usually the case of a marriage being performed without the *consent* of the Church.

- A "marriage" ceremony could also be a future, rather than a present agreement, making it more a "betrothal" - a promise of support. This may be such a vow, depicted.

- The woman is holding up her dress - why?

- It was the fashion for wealthy women to have very long dresses (German influence), which they had to hold up...but only when walking...so why, in the room?

- Is she pregnant? (This has been a long debated issue.)

- (This painting is very similar in style to another famous work *called The Marriage of the Virgin*, which represents a genre of images that depicted the Virgin Mary, very obviously pregnant, preparing for her marriage to Joseph. It is very possible that Eyck is *alluding* to such images, suggesting that the young banker's daughter was pregnant before her marriage. This may explain the need for secrecy.)

- The man wears a fur-trimmed cloak, a sign of prosperity.

- A broad hat was usually the fashion for formal occasions.

- Shoes/slippers are not worn.

- It was a local custom, some say, for a man to give his bride a gift of clogs.

- It could be that the biblical tradition of removing one's shoes when walking on sacred ground is being alluded to here, for the marriage, however secretive, would still be considered performed before God.

- Some suggest this is a sign of relaxed domesticity, even inferred sexual familiarity (his reveal dirt from outside).

- The bed: red is the most expensive dye.

- Blankets/curtains were often part of a woman's dowry.

- The bed itself, and also the colour, may symbolize carnal knowledge.

- The statues which act as finials on the chair behind the bed are of St. Margaret emerging from dragon's mouth:

  (She is said to have triumphed over the dragon)

  (She became a martyr, being beaten/tortured to death for disobeying male authority)

  (She became the patron saint of childbirth.)

- Disobeying male authority and pregnancy are thus emphasized. Coincidence?

- The brush hanging by the bed suggests "living over the brush" - domesticity.

- The dog often a woman's companion, symbolizes fidelity. "Fido" Latin for "I am faithful."

- Fruit by the window suggests, to some, a wedding gift (e.g., "good luck" for fertility)...

- but it could just as easily allude to the fruit of the Tree of Knowledge picked by Eve, i.e., "original sin." Early traditions assumed that Eden could be regained through marriage & pious faith.

- The berry bush outside the window is a subtle yet common symbol of fertility.

- Only one candle in ornate chandelier? (Poverty? Hardly)

- It is lit in daylight and is therefore special.

- Some suggest a candle indicates an official, legal act...

- ...or a divine presence (symbolized by Light...but the candle is not lit!).

- Usually, the marriage candle was carried to the church in the bridal procession. Here, it is not.

- There is also a sexual connotation: in Roman tradition, the candle was snuffed out to indicate the *consummation* of the marriage...*this* candle is no longer lit.

- Look at the beads on the wall. A sign of wealth...

- ...or a rosary, a sign of piety?

- The signature on the back wall is a cross between graffiti and the notarization of a legal document.

- The signature reads "Jan van Eyck was here, 1434."

- Was this a signal to "powers that be" that the artist was truly there...as a legal witness (e.g., was he on one of his "secret missions," to make certain the two were married?)

- In the mirror we can see that there are only two witnesses, no guests, etc.

- Miniature paintings around the mirror depict the Passion of Christ.

- Mediaeval doctrine held that all sacraments result from Christ's Passion and that a good wife will be expected to live like a Christian martyr (hence the St. Margaret allusion?)

Looking at the entire image again, note the following:

- The hand positions...are his in a gesture of taking a vow? X-ray tests show that Eyck originally had the man's hand facing the viewer, not the woman...what would that indicate?

- Her palm is up, in the manner of a submission?

- Her palm is up, in the manner of a submission?

- The use of right to left handed gestures indicated an unorthodox marriage...

- ...either to signify inheritance rights were being forfeited, or a clandestine union.

- The man is by the window, has outdoor shoes, is involved in foreign trade, adventure, etc.

- She has indoor shoes, stands near the bed, and is more confined (because she is pregnant?)

Put all this together and what do you get? A portrait of a secret wedding, perhaps, between two wealthy young friends of the Duke of Burgundy whose passion has, it seems, overtaken them. The woman is pregnant with this man's child...or, maybe, even someone else's, but he is making an honest woman of her. Up to this point, perhaps, she has been confined, to hide her "condition," which is why the wedding must take place in her rooms, and why a Church wedding is not condoned. She is under the watchful gaze of St. Margaret, both as an aid to childbirth, and as a reminder of her imposed "martyrdom" (for her "sins"?).

The painter, whose penchant is for subjects who harbour inner secrets, remember, and whose secret missions on behalf of the Duke of Burgundy make him effectively a "spy," acts as a witness to the marriage, and the painting may even be sent back to the Duke as proof of the proceedings.

This interpretation (and there can be several alternative interpretations, of course) says nothing of the politics of the time, e.g., the sexist preconceptions, etc., but that would be material relevant to an in-depth analysis of an historical theme, using the painting as an illustration, perhaps. I just wanted to take you through the breakdown of the picture itself. You can see just how much information can be gleaned from one painting. Were you to be writing a paper on this particular image, you would have enough information to construct a twenty-page essay; this can be done for any work of art or architecture.

One way to approach this type of assignment is to follow these simple steps:

❖ Look up the artist's biography and try to place the painting, etc., in context (e.g., time of life, cultural setting, etc.). Use the questions provided above.

❖ Get a clear, large, colour image of the work - a photocopy perhaps, that you can use as a reference.

❖ Take a good, hard look at the work as a whole, making only rudimentary mental notes about its content, theme, style.

❖ Cut out a centre square from a piece of plain paper, perhaps two inches square. Scan the image in a methodical way, searching for detail otherwise missed. Make a note of what you find.

❖ In a suitable dictionary of symbols, myths, etc., look up any objects you think may have significance (e.g., the berries, the candle. In terms of architecture, look for carvings, statues, decorations, shapes). Record what you find in note form.

❖ When you have analyzed each section of the image, return to the full view and compare the various findings to each other - is the symbolism fairly consistent? (It is for the *Marriage* painting, isn't it?)

❖ Reevaluate the entire picture in light of what you now know.

Chapter 7: Writing a Philosophy Paper

Almost every undergraduate in the Humanities takes a Philosophy course...or at least they should! Learning how to think logically, how to argue your case effectively, and how to expand your own thought processes are reason enough...besides, it can be great fun. As good old Will Shakespeare said: "...there are more things in heaven and earth...than are dreamt of in your philosophy..." - that means there is no end to ideas and possible "realities"!

Although I tend to get carried away when I get involved in philosophical discussions, I appreciate (now) the need for restraint during the "formative years" - if you have the flair and the imagination to contribute to lively debates in class, you will gain confidence, for sure, but if you lack the discipline, as I did at first, to formulate coherent arguments and accept constructive criticism, you will not excel in the grades department. Anyone can "soapbox" their way through a class discussion, but few can translate their passion into a reasoned, well constructed proposition on paper. The following is a three-step guide to doing just that.

Step One: Know Your Topic

❑ Explore the issue in hand: you need to fully understand your topic, which implies that it has been reduced from a sprawling, ungainly generalization, to a specific concept.

    ✓ Try to comprehend the issue from both sides of the argument before you begin to write.

    ✓ Read other people's works on the subject, to gain a broader view.

    ✓ Discuss your ideas with someone else and ask them to challenge everything you say; provide a rationale for all your statements or assumptions.

    ✓ Consider the argument by analogy (using the "what if..." scenario), by example (can you describe any precedents that would offer weight to your argument?), and by authority (can you cite reliable sources that will provide a sense of gravitas?)

    ✓ Try using the simple technique of checking the validity of your argument:

> If A then B
>
> A
>
> Therefore, B

This is called a hypothetical syllogism; if your basic argument follows this logical sequence, you can feel confident that you can progress to the next step.

❑ Consider any potential rebuttals to your argument: in philosophical debates, on paper or in class, the best strategy is defense, not offence, so when the "opposition" calls something into question, be ready to justify and defend your claims.

❑ Are there any alternatives to your own conclusion? Although your premises may be well supported, and your conclusion valid, is there another assessment of the argument that could turn out to be just as legitimate? Will you consider changing your focus?

Step Two: Develop A Functioning Outline

❑ Start with a blank piece of paper and create a mind-map, like the one described earlier (when we discussed the short story). Brainstorming is vital.

❑ In the centre of the page, write your entire claim in one, short sentence, and circle it, creating a "cell." For instance, you may be arguing that the rise of artificial intelligence has created a necessity for a new Bill of Rights, or a new concept of the term "race," etc. Write: "AI changes cultural perceptions."

❑ Branching out from this, create other "cells" that relate to the significance of your claim, e.g., any useful information collected from Step One (precedents, citations, rebuttals, etc.).

❑ Next, number the cells according to their importance. Define which articles constitute your premises, and which your supporting material (use a different colour pen, or write "P" for one, "S" for the other, etc.). Don't be too pedantic, as things can always be shifted about a bit. This is just to help you see the overall pattern of your argument...if there is one. Sometimes *this* is the process that reveals any wayward tendencies! "If in doubt, leave it out" is still a good adage, but it may also be the case that you simply don't have enough supporting information to sway your reader.

❑ Transcribe the numbered "cells" into a list.

❑ Keeping in mind how long a paper you are intending to construct, separate the main premises, creating, in effect, paragraph leaders. Supporting elements shouldn't exceed three or four per paragraph, preferably fewer. A two-page paper will have five or six paragraphs, including your Thesis Statement and Conclusion. A long paper, however, may have dozens of paragraphs, so you don't want to spend all your time on this stage, you just want to break your information down into workable, coherent units...perhaps entire sections, or even chapters. You can use the same sort of linear setup I described earlier.

❑ There will be some elements that you will want to disregard. Philosophy instructors are notorious for being ruthless when it comes to marking papers, so be ruthless with *yourself* now. Don't keep every thought, every scrap of evidence...be discerning and weed out what is weak.

❑ Remember, the Thesis Statement and Conclusion can and should be amended after the body of the essay is written. You will never create a perfect version of either *before* you write, as your phrasing in each must reflect that presented by the text...logically and metaphorically speaking, you cannot encompass an object without first having the object there, to be encompassed, and this is precisely what the TS and Conclusion do. At the outline stage, you only need a "working TS," so you can remain focused; leave the polishing to last.

❑ One of your paragraphs (at least) should pertain to rebuttals, challenges, other perceptions, etc.

Step Three: Write the Essay

❑ Follow your outline. If your essay appears to be going off the subject, or you lose your train of thought, go back to it.

❑ If you find that your perspective and/or understanding is actually changing as you write (which is quite common and shows that you are working constructively with the material), don't simply discard your outline - adapt it. Think of it as a scaffold, supporting you as you work: removing it while you are at the most critical moment will not free you, or help you...it will jeopardize everything you've done. If you need, to, though, go back to the brainstorming stage and start all over. As long as you have a consistently erected scaffold, you can build a strong argument.

❑ Keep your introduction brief and to the point. "This paper will present the argument that..." is a little stiff, perhaps, but, from my own experience, Philosophy instructors much prefer this method to some rhapsodic description of what inspired you to choose this topic, etc.

❑ You may want to include the hypothetical syllogism tactic, covering the key steps in your argument: "The main argument will be that if A, then B. A. Therefore, B." This allows your readers to follow your presentation more easily.

❑ Include a little background information to set the context of your argument. This can be an historical anecdote, a review of an article, etc., but again, keep it succinct.

❑ Use consistent terms and parallel phrasing to link paragraphs to premises. For instance, if your last sentence in one paragraph was: "It would seem that AI has forced us to reexamine the cultural status quo." Your next paragraph will begin with something like: "One of the aspects of western culture that will need reexamining is the concept of slavery." The parallel phrasing centres on the term "reexamining." Consistent terms really relate to definitions, jargon, and other specific terms that must be used in the same contexts each time - any shift in context or meaning must be explained.

❑ Always write in the third person, which is direct and neutral. Personal bias is best left out of serious Philosophy paper, unless otherwise required.

❑ Clarify statements by making them appear connected to each other and to flow smoothly. This is where *drafts* come into play. Put your first draft aside for a few days (if you have time, which you should, really), then read it over and judge for yourself if every point is clear and linked to the one preceding and/or following.

❑ When focusing on potential objections to your argument, remember to stay objective, to be respectful, and to reveal your opponent's perspective in the best possible light...the better you make the challenge sound, the stronger your argument must appear in order to refute it.

❑ Never include new information in your closing paragraph.

❑ End with an objective statement such as: "This paper has shown that..." or "It would seem to be the case, therefore, that...." Personal bias, especially at this point, will weaken your conclusion(s).

❑ When you think you have finished your final draft, think again. Have it proofread; you will be so engrossed in your own thoughts, your determination to present a sound argument, etc., you will probably have overlooked some simple elements of grammar or syntax, etc. As with the Law, which, recall, used to be the other side of the coin to Philosophy, a word written in error could lose you the entire case. Be careful.

Overall Tips

✓ Make sure your premises and conclusions are clearly defined.

✓ Present your thoughts in a natural and coherent manner, but refrain from offering subjective comments.

✓ Premises should be succinct and valid.

✓ Use concrete, specific language. Never try to wax poetical, and never use rhetorical questions...a pet peeve of every Philosophy instructor I have encountered!

✓ Loaded language, that is, language whose sole function is to bias the reader in some way, be it racist, gender oriented, hyperbolic, etc., should be avoided at all costs. Your argument and supporting evidence should be strong enough without psychological "tricks" like this.

✓ Try to give each premise (paragraph) the same degree of attention - one weak point can bring your argument tumbling down.

"A philosopher is a man who makes the best of a bad job. Socrates is called a philosopher because he didn't worry much when he was poisoned."

"Philosophy increases thirty-two feet per second."

Example

This essay demonstrates several points I have made concerning assignments, research, essay skills, and argumentation. It is a Philosophy of Science paper I co-wrote with one of my students.

Some of the elements to make note of include:

- the number of citations - a good paper has *at least* three or four per page, on average

- the use of our own ideas in conjunction with secondary sources to arrive at a thesis (i.e., that a statement made by one person can be proven to be false)

- the introductory paragraph that contains both the thesis statement *and* the proposed set up of the paper to follow

- the definition and consistent use of key words and ideas

- the integration of quotations into the text

Truth-Seekers and Self-Deception

The "love of truth" does not necessarily involve any kind of "deception," as Feyerabend would have us believe, for there are at least two distinct perceptions of "truth" and the potential attaining of it, namely, the rationalist and the empiricist perceptions. By comparing these alternative views, and by understanding how Einstein's "truth-seeking" approach blends the two, it will be shown that Feyerabend's objection is unsubstantiated.

Rationalism, exemplified by the philosophy of Plato/Socrates and Descartes, holds that certain knowledge, i.e., absolute truth, can be attained through reason alone.[1] Plato, for instance, argues for a world that is divided into the sensible realm, or "appearance," and the intelligible realm, or "reality," with the former being a source of nothing more than circumstantial/casual "opinion" and the latter a source of unchanging, universal "Truth." This distinction is made clear in the analogy of the cave, in which the inhabitants of a cave perceive mere shadows on the wall to be "reality," unaware that *beyond* the cave are forms that have cast these shadows. The world of "appearance" (e.g., that of the cave inhabitants) is but an inaccurate emulation of the world of "forms." Escaping from the cave (e.g., from the sensible world of "opinion") is the only route to enlightenment, according to Socrates, and the intellectual journey toward the "forms" is seen as an inevitable journey back to some race-memory of perfection.

This concept of humanity possessing some form of innate knowledge is reflected in the argument set forth by Descartes, in which he claims that in order for us to exist in a rational world in which we are not constantly being deceived by our falsified, and use this to gauge other "truths." This, he declares is the basic fact that if a person can think, he/she must exist. Believing such a clear and distinct consciousness to be an intuitive link to universal truths, Descartes promotes the senses, we have to discover one simple, intellectual "truth" which cannot be Platonic perspective.

Empiricism, on the other hand, contends that any, if not all "truth" comes from sensory experience. In 17th Century England, commercial and industrial interests were paramount, science had as its chief duty the task of developing

---

[1] Additional information regarding rationalism and empiricism is attributed to the following sources: Philipp Frank, *Philosophy of Science: The Link Between Science & Philosophy* (Englewood, NJ: Prentice, 1957) and Richard Popkin & A.Stroll, *Philosophy Made Simple*, 2nd ed. (New York: Doubleday, 1993).

hypotheses which satisfied the needs of society, and any theory of "knowledge" or "truth" merely had to reflect the actual achievements of the scientists. There was no place for out of reach, incomprehensible "universals." Locke, for example, argues that the mind contains no innate knowledge and must rely upon sensory observation and subsequent reflection to account for any knowledge we think we have. Taken one step further, Hume, ever the skeptic, would claim that the apparent resolution of random experiences into coherent patterns is no more than a "habit" of human nature. We cannot know if such patterns exist beyond our sensory limitations, or would continue to do so indefinitely, thus, Hume concludes, we are probably deluded if we consider ourselves privy to *any* truth at all. One concession, he grants, is that the empirical view offers itself up to the test, e.g., falsification, whereas the rationalist conception of "ultimate truths" does not.

Einstein's quest for "truth," we must observe, is a curious and profound blend of rationalism *and* empiricism, in which he ascribes to a Platonic perception of graduating degrees of "truth" and reality, while at the same time promoting an empirical, scientific process of discovery. He alludes to the quest to find proof of some "pre-established harmony", which can be likened to the Platonic quest for enlightenment with respect to the "Forms," and he perceives this ultimate reality as being observable, if only to a limited degree, through flashes of intuition.[2] He is not alone in this optimism, for Khun would agree, given that his discussion on the progress of science includes "paradigm shifts" - alternative perceptions instigated by a form of intuition.[3] Similarly, Brown's argument for the validity of thought experiments rests on the premise that the "eye of the mind" can perceive abstract patterns, and that the intellect can rationalize these into scientific laws.[4] These leaps of faith, or what Einstein calls "creative acts,"[5] offer the scientist a new perspective on reality and help to advance the "collective intellect's" escape from the realm of "opinion" (i.e., escape from Plato's cave).

[2] Albert Einstein, "Principles of Research" in *Reader* 54.

[3] Thomas Kuhn, "Revolutions as Changes of World View" 82.

[4] James Brown, "Thought Experiments Since the Scientific Revolution" 51.

[5] Einstein, "Principles" 54.

It is the relative successes of this *application* of "insight" to everyday problems that Hacking suggests makes science functional - that makes scientific "truths" a possibility[6]; even the empiricist Locke felt the need to explain the progression of science in terms of a string of intuitions. However, these successes are planted firmly in the empirical realm; they are successes of observation and measurement, successes of the scientific method. Like Medawar, who suggests that scientists can *seek* for ultimate truths but must always realize that they can see it only partially,[7] Einstein acknowledges the pragmatic requirements and limitations of science, yet, at the same time, he yearns to see the greater pattern. It is the *search* for ultimate truth that Einstein sees as being "precious," not its possession, for none can say what such a truth might be.[8] Einstein does not profess to know and, therefore, cannot be said to be self-deceived, nor to be deceiving others - he merely enjoys the journey.

Successes in science, so Einstein contends, reflect an ability to discern connections between objects and events, space and time, yet it is upon these small victories that humanity has built its apparent understanding of the dynamics of Nature, an understanding which seems to defy limitation, however prolonged its advance.[9] The more that is understood, the more scientists apply that (pragmatic) knowledge (i.e., scientific truth) to further experimentation, etc., in the hope of perceiving some simple, grand "order" that explains everything (e.g., the "pre-established harmony"). This quasi-religious quest, Einstein writes, runs the risk of "falling a prey to illusions" only if it fails to reveal the "rationality made manifest in existence."[10]

---

[6] Ian Hacking, "Experimentation and Scientific Realism" 110

[7] Peter Medawar, "The Scientific Process" 39. Cf. Popper ("Science: Conjectures and Refutations" 61), who claims that "no scientific theory can ever be deduced from observation statements," thus implying that without intuition, no absolute "truths" can be discovered.

[8] Albert Einstein, *Out of My Later Years* (New Jersey: Citadel, 1973) 110.

[9] Einstein, *Later Years* 27.

[10] Einstein, *Later Years* 29. It may be prudent to question the so-called "religious" aspect of Einstein's "pre-established harmony": It seems to be the case that it is the search,

Validated by experience, partial successes increase humanity's *potential* for attaining an ideal, e.g., ultimate "Truth"; "...hardly anyone could be found who would deny these partial successes and ascribe them to human self-deception."[11] So long as a distinction is acknowledged between ultimate truth and pragmatic, scientific truths, Einstein cannot be found at fault for suggesting such a quest is valuable.

Feyerabend, in his remark that "the love of truth is one of the strongest motives for deceiving oneself and others," fails to delineate between these two perceptions of "truth," thus weakening his argument. Scientific "truths" are, by their very definition, empirically based and, as such, are ambiguous and ever-changing: Constantly, one scientific construction is rendered inadequate and is replaced by another, and the "truths" by which we live our lives from day to day, are adapted to suit.[12] Feyerabend, according to Stevenson, claims that such constructions "cannot be rationally compared for truth," because they retain their status (i.e., of "truth") only within one system, or tradition,[13] and when that system changes, "truths" change, thus proposing, in effect, that any quest for certain knowledge, or absolute "truth" is nothing but conceit and folly.[14] Feyerabend fails to distinguish between what constitutes a change in "truths" within a tradition, and what constitutes a

---

the quest which is religious in nature, in that it is so passionate, so devoutly followed, yet, the *actual* "harmony" is quite materialistic, empirical, for it is (at least for Einstein) a simple "starting point" of physics - the singularity at the beginning of the universe. This *can* be likened to a "god" but not in the traditional sense.

[11] Einstein, *Later Years* 27.

[12] Einstein ("Principles" 54) suggests that at any one time one scientific system proves itself "superior" to the rest, which has been the case throughout history (e.g., Darwinism supersedes Creationism, the Copernican system ousted the Ptolemaic, etc.), yet Feyerabend refutes this.

[13] Leslie Stevenson, "Is Scientific Research Value-neutral?" 121.

[14] Cf. Dennis Dieks (in "The Scientific View of the World," 101), who says, "Feyerabend claims...that it is actually a mistake to think that there is one all-embracing scientific world picture."

change of tradition.[15] Therefore, his bold statement that those who love "truth" are deceived, requires some amendment.

Feyerabend would have been more accurate, perhaps, if he had stated that the love of *power* motivates deception. He suggests that at any given time, scientific truth is dictated by subjective world views and perceived priorities, thus it is malleable and potentially deceiving.[16] This is proved by historical record and Stevenson would certainly concur with this, in that he argues against the tyranny of corporations, etc., over the scientific community (e.g., imposing their own priorities, rather than supporting the general advancement of scientific thought.[17] This power, stemming from the successes of applied science, tarnishes the aspirations of theoretical scientists, such as Einstein, in that all "truths" are then seen as corruptible, when in fact, the rationalist would argue that the world of "ultimate Truth" and the world of "scientific truth" are so far removed as to make any comparison a moot point.[18]

Ambiguous as it is, scientific "truth" is all that is required to perform scientific experiments. There are no absolute, unequivocal "truths" which guide scientists - though some, such as Einstein, obviously find their task more enjoyable, more productive, perhaps, if they subscribe to some semi-philosophical/religious quest. In fact, it may be *due* to such a conviction that some scientists prove more successful than others, for it is, ultimately, a willingness to accept that there is more to the universe than we can presently comprehend that keeps scientists intrigued, and keeps them humble.[19]

If they accept their empirical findings as ultimate reality, as "certain knowledge" their careers will soon be over, for if something is "certain" it needs no

---

[15] Stevenson 122. This can be compared to Kuhn's description (in "Revolutions as Changes of World View" 85) of the "Gestalt flip" or "paradigm shift."

[16] Paul Feyerabend, "Has the Scientific View of the World a Special Status?" 65.

[17] Stevenson 120-121.

[18] Cf. Osiander's argument (105)!

[19] Richard Feynman, "The Value of Science" 31.

further experimentation,[20] yet, if they work only to attain some ideal, some nirvana-like complex of "ultimate Truths," they will fall "prey to illusion" as Einstein predicts.[21]

It seems to be the case, then, that by combining both rationalistic and empiricist perceptions of knowledge and "truth," Einstein can retain the wonder and awe that had inspired him to become a scientist in the first place, and at the same time, develop a profound respect for the scientific method and the necessity for empirical observations. Any contention Feyerabend may have with Einstein's aspiration to find a "pre-established harmony" is jeopardized by Feyerabend's own limitations (e.g., of imagination, definition, etc.). Science *can* be performed without any risk of deception, so long as it is understood that it deals only with the observable world, not with intangible "universals," and just so long as political/institutional priorities are curbed and biases recognized.

Bibliography

Brown. James R. "Thought Experiments Since the Scientific Revolution." *Reader* 45-52.

Dieks, Dennis. "The Scientific View of the World." *Reader* 95-104.

Einstein, Albert. *Out of My Later Years.* New Jersey: Citadel, 1973.

_____ . "Principles of Research." *Reader* 53-54.

Feyerabend, Paul. "Has the Scientific View of the World a Special Status Compared with Other Views?" *Reader* 63-70.

Feynman, Richard P. "The Value of Science." *Reader* 29-33.

Hacking, Ian. "Experimentation and Scientific Realism." 107-116.

Kuhn, Thomas S. "Revolutions as Changes of World View." *Reader* 79-91.

Medawar, Peter B. "The Scientific Process." *Reader* 37-43.

Osiander. "Preface to the *De Revolutionibus Orbium Coelestium* of Copernicus." *Reader* 105.

---

[20] Cf. Medawar (43), who suggests that self-criticism of scientists and their deductions is necessary and is potentially the strongest weapon they have against delusion and over-confidence.

[21] Paul Thagard, in "Why Astrology is a Pseudoscience" (72), argues that scientific theories are verifiable only if they can be used to predict results that can be measured empirically; like Hume, Thagard suggests that idealistic, or wholly Platonic concepts prohibit such testing.

Philipp, Frank. *Philosophy of Science: The Link Between Science and Philosophy*. New Jersey: Prentice, 1957.

Popkin, Richard, and A. Stroll. *Philosophy Made Simple*. 2nd ed. New York: Doubleday, 1993.

Popper, Karl R. "Science: Conjectures and Refutations." *Reader* 57-61.

Reader: *Problems in the Philosophy of Science: A Reader for Philosophy 134E.*

Stevenson, Leslie. "Is Scientific Research Value-neutral?" *Reader* 119-124.

Thagard, Paul, R. "Why Astrology is a Pseudoscience." *Reader* 71-75.

It's not a perfect paper, but it did receive an 89% grade. Although the essay contains no *formal* rebuttal, in this instance it was difficult to think of one, as every source we read suggested the same thing - Feyerabend simply got his wires crossed! We did, though, offer a little relief by suggesting a way in which he might have improved his argument...sometimes this qualifies as, or works just as well as a rebuttal. When you can't think of what the other side of the argument may be, or how to present it logically, try being ever so helpful by offering your philosophical sparring partner(s) a little kindly advice - at least it makes you come across as a gracious and well informed opponent, rather than a verbal bully! It's just like a critique in that sense.

The main thing to remember is to keep the paper tight – I tended to fly off in all directions, trying to prove that I had read certain books, and had considered every possibility, but my papers suffered for it! Most Philosophy instructors would rather see a rather dull, systematic paper that revealed a true understanding of the case in hand, than a flowery, lofty, 'show-off' piece of writing that misses the point.

CHAPTER 8: EXAMS

CHAPTER 8: EXAMS

Long before your exam you need to prepare your resources and your mind! Perhaps the most effective way of doing this, I have discovered, is to use visual stimuli, such as flash cards. You make your own, and they can be as simple or as ornate as you like - some students draw little pictures on them to help jog a memory - an image they can easily conjure up again when needed.

Card Notation for Revision

♦ Purchase one or two packets of PLAIN (not lined) index cards.

♦ As you review your notes, the course outlines, etc., make a mind-map of the following information, assigning a number to each cell:

    ✓ Topic heading (one separate card)

    ✓ Individual subject headings (e.g., authors, overall themes, etc.), which are used to present information (one card each)

    ✓ The main point of the argument, the main characteristic or purpose of a character, a one-word description of the tone of the story, etc. Highlight, or write in coloured pen.

    ✓ About 5 main points which summarize the information.

♦ You can also add:

    ✓ 1 or 2 examples, for inclusion in your answers.

    ✓ Your own relevant point (limit to 1 or 2 per heading)

♦ The number of cells per subject heading should not exceed 10 (6-7 is best). Limit your information to key words only. If using a sentence, omit words such as "the," "and," etc.

♦ Don't use quotations unless specifically advised to use these in your exam.

78

♦ Keep information succinct and general.

♦ Write on the index cards, clearly and in large letters (print), the information contained in each cell of your mind-map. One point per card. On the backs of these cards write, in pencil, the topic heading, subject heading and the number allotted to the information cell. This will be for your reference, should you mix them up and forget where the cards belong!

♦ When you have the information on the cards, find a large, flat surface (table, floor, etc.), where you can lay them out as a giant mind-map. Take your time and cast your eye over the cards - look for obvious repetitions of words, themes, ideas. Have several coloured pens, or stickers, at hand, and assign one colour for each pattern you observe. For instance, if you see the word "jealousy" crop up several times in your breakdown of Shakespeare's plays, use green to mark the corner of each card containing that word/idea. Blue could denote "honesty," and "yellow" irony, etc.

♦ Keep your cards in a plastic box, in their appropriate order, for now.

♦ Whenever you have five or ten minutes (hopefully, several times a day!), take these out and glance at them - like FLASH CARDS. Don't mull them over, don't change anything. Just allow your mind to absorb the information little by little.

♦ Every now and then, repeat the process of laying the cards out, and follow the pattern of the coloured marks, so that you can store this overall observation in your memory.

♦ As you progress, you will find that you begin to anticipate the material on the next card. Now is the time to start mixing the cards up!

♦ Use your discretion - if you are studying History, for example, don't mix the Second World War cards with the First World War cards; if you are working on Shakespeare, keep the tragedies separate from the comedies. The point is to stop your mind getting too used to one order of presentation...in an exam situation, you won't know what information you will need until you start writing - and then it will largely be a case of instant recall.

♦ If you have trained your memory to follow only one specific pattern of information, you will waste valuable time in the exam trying to relocate material. First, you memorize the information (N.B. UNDERSTANDING the material is half the battle! Remembering something you enjoy or comprehend is so much easier!), then you teach your brain how to manipulate it so the moment you see a "clue" in the exam question, one of your cards will pop into your head. This may not be the first one in the original sequence, though; during the course of the exam, as you get more information circulating in your mind, other cards will come into "view." You will need to be able to recognize where in the mind-map this fits, and how you can use it coherently. This may sound rather daunting, but really, your mind does all the work it needs to do just through the repetition of familiar stimuli. It is almost a subliminal process. All you have to do is provide kernels of information, several times a day.

♦ Juggle the cards. Play "Patience" with them, placing each card in its appropriate place, one at a time.

♦ Separate each set of cards. Lay down one, then try to guess the next in sequence.

♦ Start from the back of the deck - retrace your thoughts.

♦ Take out only the colour-coded cards. Mix up all those of one colour, then try to name where each one belongs *and* try to think of how you could use these to show an overall pattern - make up a silly story, to help you remember the order of events.

♦ Remember that the only way these cards can help your revision is if you maintain a regular and frequent use of them! You only need a few minutes each time - you don't need to review all the cards each session - just a few at a time. Five minutes' revision like this, 4 or 5 times a day, for two weeks prior to an exam, is worth more to you than countless hours of rereading, swatting, extra note-taking and consequent late nights and fatigue.

♦ A tool is only as good as the craftsman's ability to use it!

Preparing for Examinations

✓ Always rely on your note-cards when preparing for an exam.

✓ Unless you are taking a course in which details make up a significant percentage of your lecture/course material (Art History, Anthropology, History, etc), or you have been told that your exam will be open-book, you can generally expect the focus to be on generalities, overall patterns, comparisons/contrasts, etc. If you don't need to memorize a plethora of facts, don't. Make sure you have a good understanding of the broad picture, and that you have a handful of examples or general references to incorporate into your answers.

✓ Never spend valuable time memorizing quotations...if you just happen to recall one, that's fine, but it is far better that you paraphrase - an instructor wants to know that you have understood the material, not simply memorized it.

✓ Your frame of mind is just as important as your hard work, so try to keep a positive attitude as you prepare for a test - if you become anxious, try to discover where the weakness is that is causing you to have doubts about your ability. Is it because you missed several lectures and failed to catch up with the notes? Is it because you think there is so much to learn and you simply haven't the time? Finding the root of the problem is half the solution, but you must make the effort to rectify the situation in good time, e.g., ask friends, or the instructor, for an overview of the material missing; rethink your schedule and prioritize until the exam is over, etc. You need to ask yourself, "How much is this worth to me?" and act accordingly.

✓ For several days before your exam, take your cards and actively go through the various exercises described above.

✓ Always get a good night's sleep the night before the test. Worrying about anything at this stage is no more than a waste of valuable energy – it's too late to make a real difference now, so just rest and plan to be clear-headed in the morning. Try not to rely on any artificial means of getting to sleep!

✓ On the day, have a small breakfast, even if this isn't your usual routine; if you don't eat anything, a three-hour exam becomes an eternity, with your stomach rumbling every five minutes. If you eat too much, energy that should be spent of thinking is used up by the digestion, and your cognitive processes will slow down (really!).

✓ A final glance at your cards should be a cursory one - no last minute panic because you didn't memorize a particular item...no rethinking patterns or questioning meaning.

✓ Before you go into the exam, make sure you have at least two writing implements that work. Always try to use a pen, unless told otherwise. White-out pens are handy, if you tend to make lots of mistakes, though be sure your instructor hasn't banned them (some do).

✓ In the final few moments, go outside, if you can, and get some fresh air; go to the washroom, etc., but try no to talk to anyone - this is an important step for you, and you've concentrated so much on this event - it would be a shame to get distracted by chit-chat, or someone else's ideas.

✓ When you enter the room, find a place to sit where you will less likely be distracted. Sitting by the door may put you in the path of people coming in and out, or in a draught. A seat by a window may be too much of a temptation to daydream. In the middle of the class, near the front is always a good spot.

✓ You will be given you test papers in the following way: Distance Education students will be asked to show picture I.D., and to sign for their exam envelope, which will be sealed. On-campus students will often receive the answer booklets first, then the exam. The very first thing you will want to do is to jot down anything you think may help you during the exam. Did you find names a problem to memorize? Write them down on the back or in the corner of your empty sheet. The same applies to dates, sequences, key words, etc.

✓ When you are told you can begin, read over the entire exam. Decide which questions you think will be difficult, which easy. If you choose to answer the easy ones first, leave adequate space AND TIME for the questions in between. The morale boost you get from finding the first question you attack relatively simple, is helpful, but you don't want to find yourself out of time and under pressure when it comes to focusing on the essay/difficult questions. Use your discretion: balance the factors involved, e.g., time available, number of marks involved, etc. If you are really confident about the easy ones, it shouldn't take you long to jot down an answer once the major work is done.

✓ READ EACH QUESTION THOROUGHLY: precious points are lost due to lack of attention...make sure you know what is being asked of you! Always look on the reverse side!

✓ If you come to a question you simply can't answer adequately, don't leave it! Put down anything you can, even if it is in point form. Work for every potential point. You can always go back to it as new ideas crop up. Spending too much time worrying over a single question jeopardizes the rest of the exam, so move on, but don't dismiss it outright.

✓ Essay answers require a little forethought, if they are to be done well. Take a moment or two to sketch out a short outline, including an introduction, main points (broken down into paragraphs and sub-points), and a conclusion. Although spelling, handwriting and vocabulary are not the main focus of the exam, it has been proven, statistically, that the neater, better written papers receive the higher grades. For those aiming for better grades, it is well worth the effort to present a neat, well-rounded essay.

✓ Whatever you do, don't RUSH! People who leave the room early may do so for several reasons. Perhaps they are visiting the washroom, getting a drink, or quitting because they've simply had enough...if you judge yourself by other people's apparent behaviour, you will find yourself trying to compete. There is nothing wrong in being the last one to finish! Take all the time you need.

✓ When you have written all you think you can remember, go back over the exam. Re-read the questions and your answers. Is there anything else you can add? Do you see any obvious error? Will a diagram help explain your thoughts? What about that question you had no clue how to answer - any ideas now?

✓ Don't be tempted to change *everything* you feel uncertain about now you've reread your answers. Remember, your initial "gut reaction" to a question is usually right. Intuition is there for a reason   - listen to it! Use your discretion - if you tackled a problem that you found confusing, or difficult from the beginning, this is probably worth revising; if you found a question easy to answer and finished it quickly, don't change anything, but add to it any extra details you may have omitted.

✓ When you have finished, leave quietly so as not to disturb others still writing. Go and treat yourself!

"Who was Charon? Charon was the man who fried soles over the sticks."

CHAPTER 9: EXPANDING YOUR HORIZONS

I have striven not to laugh at human actions, not to weep at them, nor to hate them, but to understand them.

(Spinoza)

Suggested Reading

You need not read all of these books in order to have a good cross-section of background material, they are merely examples of the types of material you should find useful throughout your University career. The more you read, the more you have to include in your own writing and this is always beneficial (be wary of using quotations or direct references if you have only limited understanding of a work, though, for you may use these incorrectly). You may want to make yourself a reading list for your holidays - just one book at a time.

Becket (Tennyson) and/or **Murder in the Cathedral** (Eliot)
Old Testament (Genesis, Exodus, Job, Song of Solomon, Jeremiah, Ezekiel)
New Testament (Luke, John, Acts, Revelation)
The Prince (Machiavelli)
Candide (Voltaire)
Faust (Goethe)
The Inferno (Dante)
How Green Was My Valley (Richard Llewellyn)
David Copperfield (Dickens)
Idylls of the King (Tennyson)
Jude the Obscure (Hardy)
The Dubliners (James Joyce)
Hedda Gabler (Ibsen)
Metamorphosis (Kafka)
A Room of One's Own (Virginia Woolf)
Lady Chatterley's Lover (D. H. Lawrence)
The Confessions of St. Augustine
Brave New World (Aldus Huxley)
The Song of Roland
On Liberty (Mill)
Leviathan (Hobbes: choose sections -- "On Sovereignty" is good)
Republic (Plato: choose sections)
Metaphysics (Aristotle: choose sections)

Letter Concerning Toleration (Locke)
Tales from the Decameron (Boccaccio)
The Romance of Tristan and Iseult
Tales of King Arthur (Malory)
Rubáiyát of Omar Khayyám (Edward Fitzgerald)
The Time Machine (H. G. Wells)
The Gift of the Magi (O. Henry)
Washington Square (Henry James)
Woman in White (Wilkie Collins)
Short Stories (Guy de Maupassant)
The Crucible (Arthur Miller)
The Iliad / Odyssey

Really, anything and everything you can! The list could go on and on! Browse through the Literature section of a good book shop, or Library and experiment a bit. Try the Classics section, too (this means the Greek and Roman stuff!) - and the Philosophy and History sections - and try reading some Plays and Libretti!

Suggested Viewing

Have fun with these – don't take them too seriously with respect to information - Hollywood has a tendency to blur the facts in favour of "glitz," as you know. Even some T.V. historical dramas do the same, but these do tend to be more historically correct in the long run. What you want is a wide exposure to various periods, styles, regions and topics. If you can think of others, jot them down and make the effort to hire them on Video some time.

If you find one you really like, make the effort to watch it several times - a good film/show usually has several "layers" to it which require several viewings to fully appreciate. I have seen Kenneth Branagh's *Hamlet* five times (it's four hours long, which makes that twenty hours' worth!) - the first time I was just overawed, the second time I picked up more of the underlying story of the battle going on in the background, the third time I followed it in the text to see if it varied from the original at all, the fourth, I sat back and just enjoyed the actual performances, the costumes, the fighting scenes, etc. The fifth, I began to really analyze what Shakespeare was saying through the different characters - little nuances came to light, as did subtle visual clues that you simply don't get with a flat reading.

(British History)

Lady Jane (Young Queen executed)
A Man for All Seasons (Paul Scofield as Sir Thomas More - brilliant)
The Lion in Winter (Kate Hepburn & Peter O'Toole - brilliant!)
Elizabeth (1998)
Orlando (Varius [early] periods, Virginia Woolf - brilliant visuals)
Hamlet (1998 Kenneth Branagh's version)
Henry V (Kenneth Branagh)
BBC productions of Shakespeare's plays (recently completed entire repertoire)
Ivanhoe (Early Britain)
Rob Roy (Early Britain)
Robin Hood (Any good, serious version)

(Of course, any of the new BBC adaptations of literary classics like **Far from the Madding Crowd** [Hardy]; **Our Mutual Friend** and other Dickens' books; **Pride & Prejudice** and other Jane Austen works; E.M. Forster's **A Room With a View**, **Howard's End**, etc. Keep your eye open for T.V. specials and look around the video store. Although not specifically "Historical," these can offer you great insight into their respective periods, class-structures, political/social contexts, etc.).

(European/Russian History)
The Man in the Iron Mask (Louis XIV)
Les Miserable (French Revolution)
The Count of Monte Cristo (French, late 17th early 18th Century)
Luther (Protestantism)
Galileo Galilei (Obvious!)
The Agony and the Ecstacy (for Michelangelo fans)
A Tale of Two Cities (French Revolution)
Rasputin (Russian "Healer")
Hermitage/ St. Petersburg (Peter Ustinov's series)
Amadeus (Mozart)
Dr. Zhivago (Russian Revolution)
Shoes of the Fisherman (Choosing a Pope)

(Classical)
Oedipus the King (Sophocles)*   * Usually BBC productions - check Library
Antigone (Sophocles)*
Hippolytus (Euripides)*
Agamemnon (Aeschylus)*
Prometheus Bound (Aeschylus)*
Jason and the Argonauts / Golden Fleece

Cleopatra (Elizabeth Taylor - glitzy but fascinating)
I Claudius (Roman Empire)
Spread of the Eagle (Roman Empire)
Spartacus (Kirk Douglas - Greece)
The Odyssey (Greek legend)
Alexander the Great (Richard Burton)
Helen of Troy (Self-explanatory)
Last Days of Pompeii (Self-explanatory)
Ben Hur (Roman Empire)

(Biblical)
Mystery Plays* (Sometimes on TV near Christmas time)
Ben Hur (Roman context)
The Ten Commandments (Self-explanatory, epic)
The Greatest Story Ever Told (Epic)
The Robe (Crucifixion aftermath)
Jesus of Montreal (Great symbolism)
The Last Temptation of Christ (Alternative view, but not so controversial now)
The Life of Brian (Monty Python - hilarious and surprisingly accurate, historically!)
Masada ("Jews" vs. Romans)
Quo Vadis? (Peter in Rome / Christian persecution)
Salome (Death of John the Baptist, etc.)

(New World)
The Mission (Robert De Niro)
At Play in the Fields of the Lord (Missionaries)
1492 (Guess!)
Amastad (Slave Trade)
The Crucible (Salem witch trials)

(Eastern)
The Last Emperor (Rise of Communism)
Kundun (Dalai Lama)
Farewell My Concubine (Subtitles)
Seven Years in Tibet (Dalai Lama)
A Passage to India (19ᵗʰ Century Raj days)
Jewel in the Crown (T.V.)
The Little Buddha (Explains legend)
Gandhi (20ᵗʰ Century)

(War)
ANZACS (WWI - Australians)
Glory (American Civil War)
Lawrence of Arabia (WWI +)
Zulu (Self-explanatory)
Schindler's List (WWII)
Saving Private Ryan (WWII)
In Which We Serve (WWII)
All Quiet on the Western Front (WWII)
Three Came Home (WWII)
The Best Years of Our Lives (WWII)

(Films about Learning)
Educating Rita (Michael Caine & Julie Walters - funny, but poignant)
Dead Poets Society (Based on a true story)
To Sir with Love (Sydney Poitier)
Renaissance Man (Danny deVito - funny, but has its moments of insight)

Suggested Listening

When listening to recordings, do make the effort to set aside enough time to hear the entire work - interruptions are harder to overcome than when you are watching a video, etc., because your own imagination is creating the "scenes" for you. If possible, don't do anything else while you're listening, and try to relax and enjoy (dim the lights and get comfortable).

Under Milk Wood (Dylan Thomas - great language/imagery)
Paradise Lost (to help you through!)
Shakespeare's works* - English versions
Canterbury Tales*
Any Poetry!
Dickens excerpts
Jesus Christ Superstar (Get the original stage version from the Library and follow the words)
Any Opera!

"The Plebeians were a sex of the Romans."

One of the most valuable traits, or abilities, of the aspiring student is, as I said from the very beginning, eclecticism...an appreciation for a variety of subjects - history, literature, music, art, philosophy, basic scientific knowledge.

The following 200 general knowledge questions and answers are intended to inspire you to expand your horizons a bit further. Try not to peek at the answers straight away; ask someone, look it up, or get someone else to give you a "hint." Have fun!

"I Never Knew That!"

1. What is meant by "The Land of the Rising Sun?"
2. Who is supposed to have cut the Gordian Knot?
3. Who wrote *Dr. Jekyll and Mr. Hyde*?
4. Of what school of painting was Picasso a member?
5. Who was the "Bard of Avon"?
6. For what is Job particularly noted?
7. What famous composer was, at one time, the lover of George Sand?
8. What is cuneiform writing?
9. What are the primary colours (in painting)?
10. What is the original title of the Mona Lisa painting, by Leonardo da Vinci?
11. How was Cleopatra supposed to have died?
12. Under what "sign" was Constantine the Great assured victory in battle with Maxentius?
13. To what island was Napoleon banished in 1814?
14. What is a centaur?
15. Why is it that Achilles had only one vulnerable spot?
16. What are "The Dreaming Spires"?
17. Who was "The Lady with the Lamp"?
18. For what act is this a metaphor: "Thirty pieces of silver"?
19. What is meant if someone says: "You must be like Caesar's wife"?
20. Who was Queen Vashti?
21. Match the following:

Plutarch	Divine Comedy
Lamb	Salome
Dante	Lives
Darwin	Essays on Shakespeare
Wilde	Voyage of the Beagle

22. What is the Prime Mover and who wrote of it?

23. What does *in camera* mean?

24. What did the Pied Piper of Hamelin claim he could do? What did he do?

25. Who fought the Battle of Waterloo in 1815?

26. Who is responsible for developing Calculus?

27. Ptolemy defined the universe with _____ at its centre.

28. What is the Rosetta stone and where was it found?

29. What is papyrus?

30. What character in Sophocles' drama was buried alive for strewing dust over a dead warrior?

31. For what work is Edward Gibbon famous?

32. Which was known as the Dark Continent? Why?

33. What were the circumstances of the death of Sir Walter Raleigh?

34. What is the Eternal City?

35. What is a polytheist?

36. Who wrote *The Pilgrim's Progress*?

37. Who was Alexander the Great's teacher?

38. What is the Egyptian *Book of the Dead*?

39. What happened to those who looked upon the face of Medusa?

40. To what letter does Hawthorne refer in his title *The Scarlet Letter*?

41. What religious movement was instigated by Martin Luther?

42. What is the Koran?

43. Who was Xanthippe and for what was she famous?

44. What does the term "apostate" mean?

45. What are harpies?

46. What famous library of ancient times was destroyed by fire during a Roman invasion?

47. What is a saga?

48. What was the Inquisition?

49. Who was the "wandering Jew"?

50. What female chemist isolated the radioactive elements of radium?

51. What river flows through Rome?

52. Mars was the Roman god of _____.

53. Who were the Huguenots?

54. Who was the first king of Rome?

55. The high priest of Apollo, together with his two sons, was killed by serpents for his opposition to the reception of the wooden horse into Troy. This is depicted in a famous statue (now in the Vatican) called _____.

56. Who is considered Germany's greatest poet?

57. What is the Vatican?

58. What is meant by "Hobson's Choice"?

59. What event in 1605 is remembered each year in England by the burning of an effigy?

60. What is Avalon?

61. What happened to the Spanish Armada in 1588?

62. What does the abbreviation "mss" stand for?

63. What does "preclude" mean?

64. What is the famous nursery rhyme called which teaches children the names of the various bells of London?

65. What is the literal translation of Archimedes' "Eureka!"?

66. What would be meant by the phrase: "You are a Jeremiah!"?

67. Who opened King Tutankhamun's tomb in 1922?

68. From where were the Elgin Marbles taken?

69. What is the obvious difference between a Gothic arch and a Romanesque arch?

70. Who was the famous 2nd Century Greek physician to the Roman elite?

71. What does the term "Sans Culottes" mean and to whom does it refer?

72. What is the Arabic equivalent of: CMXIV ?

73. If you were an Augur in ancient Rome, what would be your job?

74. What is "The Jewel in the Crown"?

75. For what discovery is Michael Faraday famous?

76. Tchaikovsky's 1812 Overture was eventually commemorated to whose defeat?

77. From whom did the French rebels adopt their "Cap of Liberty"?

78. David painted a portrait entitled *The Death of Marat* - what does it depict and who was Marat?

79. In the counting rhyme "Tinker, Tailor, Soldier, Sailor," etc., what is meant by "Tinker"?

80. What is "erudition"?

81. What is the legend behind the motto: *"Honi soit qui mal y pense"*?

82. What is the difference between the dating terms "B.C." and "B.C.E."?

83. What is the difference between an Ionic pillar and a Corinthian pillar?

84. What is a necropolis?

85. In William Blake's "Songs of Experience" he writes:

> *Tyger, tyger, burning bright*
> *In the forests of the night.....*
> *...Did he who made the Lamb make thee?*

Explain the allusion to the "Lamb."

86. For what is Niccolò Paganini (1782-1840) famous?

87. Beethoven's "Eroica" symphony is thought to have been inspired by Napoleon - why did the composer supposedly change his mind and change the work's dedication?

88. What was the "Grand Tour"?

89. In *Gulliver's Travels*, what is meant by the statement that Gulliver is considered more like the Houyhnhnms than the Yahoos?

90. From which novel comes the well-known phrase: "It is a far, far better thing I do than I have ever done"?

91. What were known as the "humours"?

92. What is said to be "the first casualty of War"?

93. What is the name of the sacred bull worshiped by the ancient Egyptians?

94. Which famous Society features in Mozart's *The Magic Flute*?

95. Who was the Maid of Orleans?

96. The Alchemists were said to be in search of the _____ Stone.

97. "Crossing the Rubicon" is an allusion to what event and how could this be used as a metaphor?

98. What does "*in vino veritas*" mean?

99. What caused the American patriots to dump tea into Boston Harbour in 1773?

100. The Greek god of medicine is called _____.

101. What is the most familiar ancient Egyptian symbol for "Life"?

102. What is a "scapegoat"?

103. What did Percival Lowell supposedly observe on the surface of Mars?

104. Who gave us an eyewitness account of the eruption of Vesuvius and the destruction of Pompeii?

105. What are tessera?

106. Explain the phrase: "*in medias res.*"

107. Who said: "Man was born free, and everywhere he is in chains"?

108. What is the "undiscovered country" and who wrote of it?

109. The exit corridors of the Colosseum are called _____.

110. In which country was the Potato Famine?

111. Ancient Greek Theatre was originally a staged competition between two _____.

112. What is the Blarney Stone and how is it used to describe someone who speaks well (or to excess)?

113. Who wrote *The Speckled Band* and to what does the title refer?

114. What does "lilliputian" mean?

115. Who is famous for saying "Lord, make me chaste...but not yet!"?

116. Samuel Pepys is famous for writing _____.

117. Who was Emperor when Rome was set afire in the year 64?

118. Who is the Madonna?

119. What was Danegeld?

120. What is Spiritualism?

121. What are the two types of sonnet?

122. What is a *nike* and which is the famous statue now in the Louvre?

123. Who was King Arthur's illegitimate son, who instigated the downfall of Camelot?

124. Whose famous memoirs were inspired by the taste of a small, sweet cake?

125. What is a geisha?

126. Who ordered the *Doomsday Book* and what did it record?

127. In which War did Florence Nightingale gain most of her training?

128. Who built the first and second Temples in Jerusalem?

129. Who was the Sun King?

130. What happened to the painting of Dorian Gray?

131. What is the correct name for the soldiers who have guarded the Popes for 500 years?

132. What is the Creationist's belief?

133. What happened to Sodom and Gomorrah?

134. Some monks cut a circle of hair from the tops of their heads - what is this called?

135. What is an historiated capital?

136. *The Crucible* relates what event?

137. How is the Archangel Michael often depicted?

138. Who was Lily Langtry?

139. Explain a "comedy of manners."

140. What/who was "restored" at the time of the Restoration?

141. Who declared: *"Veni, vidi, vici"*?

142. What is the *Book of Kells*?

143. What happened on the "road to Damascus"?

144. What is the name of the Norse afterworld?

145. What was Robin Hood's real name?

146. In northern England between 1811-16 groups of workmen destroyed labour-saving machinery in an attempt to save their jobs. They were known as the _____, being so named after Ned Lud who, in 1779 broke up stocking frames.

147. Who demanded his "pound of flesh"?

148. Where did the term "titian red" originate?

149. What is polyphony?

150. Vestal Virgins were responsible for what?

151. Guy de Maupassant is famous for writing short stories; one of his themes is the _____ War.

152. Which came first, chronologically, Art Deco or Art Nouveau?

153. Michelangelo's final achievement was the dome of _____ in Rome.

154. What is the Golden Mean?

155. What is the section of a church/cathedral which crosses the nave?

156. What was Jude's profession in *Jude the Obscure*?

157. What is the Hindu name for the final reunion with the Brahma?

158. Niobe was punished for what act? What was her punishment?

159. In Norse mythology, the final destruction of the world in a battle between the gods and the powers of Hel led by Loki is known as Ragnarok. How is this name translated?

160. Who founded the Academy of Sciences in 1724, in St. Petersburg, as part of an attempt to bring Russia in line with European intellectual and commercial standards ?

161. Nicolaus Copernicus (1473-1543) is famous for what theory?

162. To what event does the epithet "Bloody Sunday" refer?

163. What is a spectre?

164. Icarus is known in Greek mythology for flying too close to the sun and melting his waxen wings. What, though, was the name of his father, who *made* the wings and who is recognized as the most ingenious artificer of Athens?

165. In which book do Pierre, Natasha and Andre appear?

166. Explain the use of the *"deus ex machina."*

167. What are the first five books of the Bible collectively called?

168. Why was Sir Thomas More beheaded?

169. What is a colloquialism?

170. What was the Bastille and what happened to it?

171. What was the Maginot Line?

172. What is a quisling?

173. What is a misanthrope?

174. In which Dickens novel is Mr. Bumble?

175. What were indulgences and who sold them?

176. What are "pieces of eight" and in which book are they made famous?

177. Who was Emmeline Pankhurst?

178. What "cracked from side to side" in Tennyson's "The Lady of Shalott"?

179. Explain Machiavellism.

180. What is crenelation?

181. Match the following:

Gabriel	Oliver Twist
Lazarus	Far From the Madding Crowd
Fagin	The Tempest
Caliban	Don Quixote
Sancho Panza	The Gospel According to John

182. Neoclassicism arose as a reaction against the flamboyant _____ and _____ styles of early 18ᵗʰ Century Europe.

183. What is meant by "A face to launch a thousand ships"?

184. Who was the Virgin Queen?

185. Match the following:

Anthropomorphism	He dealt them a blushing crow
Spoonerism	An honest politician
Malapropism	The leering trees frightened her
Oxymoron	He is the paramour of virtue

186. Who wrote "The Ballad of Reading Gaol"?

187. What was the scarab a symbol of in ancient Egypt?

188. If "darkness" and/or "night" were being intentionally used as symbols in a text, what would they represent?

189. In ancient times comets were often considered to be _____.

190. The Hindu god Shiva dances the Dance of _____.

191. Alexander the Great was victorious over Darius at the Battle of _____.

192. What is Sisyphus known for and why would this be a common allusion in literature?

193. What are the four Eastern philosophies?

194. What do Rationalists theorize?

195. What is a "round robin"?

196. What did the Iconoclasts do (8ᵗʰ Century)?

197. Who painted "Starry Night"?

198. What were the "Salons" of 18ᵗʰ Century France (i.e., Paris)?

199. Explain the allusion to "Damocles' sword."

200. In 14ᵗʰ Century Europe, who were the Flagellants?

Answers

1. Japan
2. Alexander the Great
3. Robert L. Stevenson
4. Post-Impressionist
5. William Shakespeare
6. His trials and his patience
7. Frederick Chopin
8. Wedge-shaped inscriptions (Assyria, Babylonia, Persia, etc.)
9. Red, blue, yellow

10. La Gioconda

11. Snake bite

12. The sign of the Cross

13. Elba

14. A mythical creature with a man's head and trunk and the rest a horse's body

15. When he was a baby, Achilles' mother had contrived to dip him into a mystical river that would make him invulnerable. However, she had to hold him by the heel, so that was the one spot untouched by the water. It was his one weakness.

16. The skyline of Oxford University - metaphor for academe

17. Florence Nightingale

18. Betrayal

19. You must be seen to be good/pure (even if you are not!)

20. The Queen in the Book of Esther who refused to present herself to the King

21. Plutarch: Lives   Lamb: Essays on Shakespeare   Dante: Divine Comedy
    Darwin: Voyage of the Beagle   Wilde: Salome

22. Aristotle's idea was that there must have been some initial force which set the universe in motion and then ceased to function.

23. In secret (e.g., behind closed doors)

24. Rid the town of rats by playing on his flute - instead, he led the children away.

25. The Duke of Wellington (England) and Napoleon (France)

26. Isaac Newton

27. The Earth

28. A piece of black basalt found near the Rosetta mouth of the Nile. Bears inscriptions in three languages (Greek, demotic characters and hieroglyphics) - used to decipher hieroglyphs.

29. Writing material made from the pressed and matted pith of a tall reed-like plant native to the Nile region.

30. Antigone

31. Writing *The Decline and Fall of the Roman Empire*

32. Africa: Little was known of it because exploration was slow - it was "mysterious."

33. He was beheaded for treason

34. Rome

35. Someone who believes in many gods

36. John Bunyan

37. Aristotle

38. A sacred text placed in the tomb to guide the spirit through the Underworld

39. They turned to stone

40. A (for Adultery)

41. Protestantism

42. The Holy Book of the Muslim religion

43. The wife of Socrates, known for her sharp tongue

44. One who forsakes, or abandons a previously held faith

45. Mythological creatures, half bird half human (female) - snatched away the souls of the dead and were generally disagreeable.

46. Alexandrian Library

47. Icelandic, mediaeval story of a hero and his family/society (historical or legendary)

48. Tribunal set up by the Catholic Church in the pursuit of heresy and the punishment of heretics

49. Supposedly a Jew who scoffed at Jesus when he stumble under his cross - he was condemned to walk the earth until the Second Coming.

50. Marie Curie

51. Tiber

52. War

53. French Protestants (weavers)

54. Romulus

55. The Laocoon

56. Johann Wolfgang Goethe

57. Originally a Roman suburb where St. Peter was supposedly buried. Pilgrimages inspired building of Basilica, the Holy Roman See of the Catholic religion. The Popes' residence.

58. Take what is offered or go without. (Hobson was an English stableman who made customers take the horse nearest the door).

59. The attempted destruction of the Houses of Parliament (England) by Guy Fawkes

60. The legendary burial place of King Arthur (Glastonbury, England)

61. Before the English fleet had time to set sail a storm destroyed much of the

Armada

62. Manuscripts

63. To exclude, render ineffectual, prevent, etc.

64. Oranges and Lemons

65. "I have found it!"

66. You are a pessimist, a harbinger of doom, etc.

67. Howard Carter

68. From the Parthenon in Athens, Greece

69. Usually, a Gothic arch is "pointed"- a Romanesque arch is not

70. Galen (used as the name of the doctor in *Planet of the Apes*!)

71. "Without Trousers" - name given to the French revolutionists

72. 914

73. You would be a member of the highest order of official diviners, soothsayers, etc.

74. India

75. Electro-magnetism

76. Napoleon

77. From the freed slaves of ancient Rome (otherwise known as Phrygian caps)

78. Depicts a man, dead in his bath. A follower of Rousseau, Jean Paul Marat was a French revolutionist murdered by Charlotte Corday in 1793.

79. A mender of pots & pans, etc.

80. Learning, especially in literature, history or criticism - scholarship

81. "Evil to him who evil thinks" - At a ball, a garter of the Countess of Salisbury, having slipped off, was picked up by the King, who expressed himself in the above phrase and fastened it around his own knee, thus refusing to cause the lady embarrassment. It became the highest order of knighthood in Britain.

82. B.C. stands for "Before Christ" and B.C.E. stands for "Before the Common Era." The latter is more commonly used in modern scholarship in order not to cause offence to non-Christians. (A.D. was "Anno Domini," or "The Year of Our Lord," but today it is better to use "C.E." – "Common Era").

83. Basically, an Ionic pillar has spiral volutes (scroll-like tops), but a Corinthian pillar has a bell-shaped capital decorated with acanthus leaves.

84. Literally "city of the dead" - a vast burial site.

85. Blake's "Songs of Innocence and Experience" record the passage from "innocent" belief in Christianity, to an "experienced" skepticism - he seems to mourn the loss of youthful "ignorance" and compares the "Tyger" (reality - pain, anger, sorrow, famine, war, etc.) to the "Lamb" (Jesus as children are taught about him)... can the two really stem from the same God?

86. Concert violinist and composer

87. Beethoven was disgusted by Napoleon crowning himself Emperor

88. A tour of Europe people of means took to enhance their education, etc.

89. This was spoken to Gulliver by the leader of the equine kingdom - he was comparing Gulliver, favourably, to the semi-human ruffians...he was more like the sophisticated horses.

90. *A Tale of Two Cities* by Charles Dickens

91. In the body: phlegm (phlegmatic), blood (sanguine), yellow bile (choleric), black bile (melancholic). Described by Galen, and made "characteristics" in mediaeval period.

92. Journalist E. R. Morrow claimed that Truth is the first casualty of War, but earlier, Innocence was said to be the victim.

93. Apis

94. The Freemasons

95. Joan of Arc

96. The Philosopher's Stone

97. Julius Caesar crossing the Rubicon River - an act which "officially" made him the enemy of the Republic. Metaphor for any irrevocable decision.

98. "In wine there is Truth."

99. They were demonstrating against raised taxes on imports from England, etc.

100. Aesculapius

101. The Ankh

102. Someone who takes the entire blame

103. Canals

104. Pliny the Younger, in his letters to Tacitus

105. Small, square pieces of glass, stone, etc., used to make mosaics

106. Literally: "In the middle of things" - used to explain that something is already in progress when you come in, join, etc.

107. Jean-Jacques Rousseau

108. The afterlife (not specifically "death"). Shakespeare (from Hamlet's "To be, or not to be..." soliloquy)

109. Vomitories (LL. *Vomitoria*)

110. Ireland

111. Poets

112. A stone in Blarney Castle, Ireland. When kissed, the stone imparts a smooth tongue...the profusion of compliments is called "blarney" e.g., "It's the blarney you're giving me," or, "You must have kissed the Blarney Stone!"

113. Sir Arthur Conan Doyle - a poisonous snake

114. Very small

115. St. Augustine

116. Diaries

117. Nero

118. The Mother of Jesus

119. An annual tax originally imposed to pay off Danish invaders

120. A belief in a spirit world (an idealism: "all that exists is spirit" - a practise: alleged communication with the dead through a medium)

121. The Elizabethan, or Shakespearean and the Italian, or Petrarchan

122. A winged Victory - the Nike of Samothrace

123. Mordred

124. Marcel Proust

125. Japanese singer/dancer

126. William the Conqueror - survey and estimate of value of all the lands in England

127. Crimean

128. The first was built by Solomon, the second, by King Herod the Great

129. Louis XIV

130. It changed to reflect all the negative thoughts and attributes of its subject, Dorian Gray, while he remained youthful and serene-looking.

131. The Swiss Guard

132. That the world was created just as it is described in the Book of Genesis, i.e., in six days

133. They were destroyed by fire and brimstone for being corrupt

134. Tonsure

135. In an illustrated manuscript of the Mediaeval period, some capital letters were ornately decorated with little scenes, including people, foliage, etc.

136. The witch trials at Salem, MA

137. As a warrior

138. English actress ("The Jersey Lily") - friend to Oscar Wilde

139. Satirical play concerned with social codes of the upper classes; plays of the Restoration period offer the most examples, but also do some works of Shakespeare, Sheridan and Wilde.

140. The re-establishment of the monarchy under Charles II (England)

141. "I came, I saw, I conquered" - Julius Caesar

142. An Irish illuminated manuscript of the Latin Gospels (c.1000 C.E.)

143. St. Paul's conversion

144. Valhalla

145. Robert, Earl of Locksley

146. Luddites

147. Shylock from Shakespeare's *The Merchant of Venice*

148. From the red-headed women in the portraits painted by Titian, the Renaissance artist

149. Literally, "many sounds." In music - simultaneous and harmonizing

150. The fire which was eternally lit within the Temple of Vesta (the god of the Hearth)

151. Franco-Prussian

152. Art Nouveau

153. St. Peter's Basilica

154. The way of wisdom and safety between extremes - moderation

155. The transept

156. Stonemason

157. Nirvana

158. She was turned to stone for boasting about her numerous children in the face of a goddess who had only two.

159. "The Twilight of the Gods"

160. Czar Peter the Great

161. That the Earth orbited the Sun and not vice versa

162. The massacre of peaceful protesters against the regime of Czar Nicholas II (1905) - ignited the Russian Revolution

163. An apparition, ghost

164. Daedalus

165. *War and Peace* by Leo Tolstoi

166. "A god from a machine" - any artificial contrivance to solve a difficulty (can be physical, as in ancient Greek theatre, or literary, etc.)

167. The Pentateuch

168. He refused the oath of the king's supremacy (over Rome and the Pope), an act which was treasonable.

169. A term, phrase, etc., used in familiar conversation - informal

170. Fortress-prison in the heart of Paris and the most hated symbol of royal power and authority, the Bastille was destroyed by Revolutionists in 1789.

171. The French line of defence in WWI

172. A traitor, especially one who becomes the tool of a conqueror of his country.

173. Someone who hates people

174. *Oliver Twist*

175. Remission of punishment in Purgatory for sins - various degrees of indulgences were sold by the Catholic Church to the faithful.

176. Spanish coins of eight reals (i.e., eight to the dollar) - *Treasure Island* by Robert L. Stevenson

177. The 19ᵗʰ Century Suffragette who threw herself under a racehorse in defiance against a law which disallowed women from voting

178. The "mirror"

179. A code of conduct whereby a ruler is justified in using any means available to secure a strong central government.

180. Battlements atop a building, usually a castle, for the purpose of providing cover to soldiers protecting the structure.

181. Gabriel: Far From the Madding Crowd   Lazarus: The Gos. Acc. to John
    Fagin: Oliver Twist Caliban: The Tempest   Sancho Panza: Don Quixote

182. Baroque / Rococo

183. Alludes to Helen of Troy's beautiful face, hence any beautiful woman.

184. Queen Elizabeth I

185. Anthropomorphism: The leering trees frightened her   Spoonerism: He dealt them a blushing crow Malapropism: He is the paramour of virtue Oxymoron: An honest politician

186. Oscar Wilde

187. The Sun god

188. Evil, suspicion, mystery, etc.

189. Portents

190. Creation

191. Issus

192. Continuously rolling a round rock up a hill - futility, perseverance against the odds, etc.

193. Taoism, Buddhism, Hinduism, Confucianism

194. Reason is a source of knowledge in itself, superior and independent of sense perception.

195. Petition signed by several people - originally signed in a circle to conceal who signed it first.

196. Destroyed images in the Byzantine churches

197. Vincent van Gogh

198. Gatherings of intellectuals and social elite, usually in the salons of wealthy estates and usually hosted by women. Debates and critiques were intended to refine intellectual skills and demonstrate the full potential of an enlightened and perfected civilization.

199. Damocles, having commented on the happiness which the tyrant Dionysus must enjoy, was invited to dine with him - he looked up and discovered a sword hanging from a single hair above his head. Used as a metaphor for impending danger, doom, etc.

200. Devout people who believed the Plague was divine retribution for sin - they walked through the country beating themselves with sticks, etc., as an act of penance.

CHAPTER 10: GODS GALORE!

Being an "A" student in the Humanities requires that you learn about the basic mythological and religious stories to which poets, authors, painters, and even composers allude. It is an ancient practise that has permeated human artistic expression since we first started telling stories around communal fires.

It is such an important but, sadly, all too often neglected aspect of our formal education nowadays, that any student who can demonstrate a familiarity with fundamental themes such as the Creation story (Old Testament), the traditions concerning Jesus, and the universal "odyssey," will undoubtedly earn higher grades than those who fail to grasp the references.

Remember, most university instructors are well versed, themselves, in all this material, and must wade through many papers every day that show no hint of recognition of some of the world's most influential concepts...how refreshing it will be for them to come across a paper that mentions mythological allusion and biblical imagery!

Just to assure you that mythological and biblical allusion is alive and well today, as it ever was, I've listed a few examples in each field. I'm sure you will be able to add a few of your own.

Mythological Symbolism/Allusion

➤ The names of the planets and their moons (in *our* solar system!) Have been named after the Roman gods and their consorts.

➤ The constellations have been named after gods, goddesses and mythological beasts.

➤ Someone's "Achilles' heel" is their weak or vulnerable spot.

➤ A beautiful young man is often called "an Adonis," or "an Apollo."

➤ "Cupid" has become the familiar symbol of St. Valentine's Day.

➤ "Rich as Croesus" is a familiar simile for the very wealthy.

➤ The "caduceus" is the recognized symbol of the medical profession.

➤ A "Herculean task" is something that requires great effort.

➤ To "rise like a Phoenix" is to be resilient and persistent.

➤ An "Oedipus complex" is a well-known psychological condition.

➤ "A face to sink a thousand ships" is an allusion to Helen of Troy - used to denote any beautiful woman.

➤ The name "psyche" is still used to identify the human mind, the individual's "soul" etc.

➤ "Bacchanalia" are drunken orgies/revelries.

➤ Europe is symbolized by the female figure, "Europa."

➤ A "Pandora's Box" is considered anything that has the potential of being dangerous, complicated, harmful, etc. Something that, once "unleashed," is difficult to stop, such as Nuclear power, etc.

➤ Some music is still described as being "Orphic" (i.e., like Orpheus' music, that can make you sleepy, or sad).

➤ "Titanic" means colossal and stems from "Titan."

➤ The movie *Pygmalion* (*My Fair Lady*) was based on the myth of Pygmalion and Galatea.

➤ To be "under Damocles' sword" is to feel pressured, to be under duress, etc. Impending calamity.

Mythological Stories & Characters

The following are listed with the Greek name unless otherwise stated (there is a list at the end of this section of the corresponding Roman names, where they exist).

Achilles

- Greek hero. Dipped, as a baby, into the river Styx, by his mother. The water was supposed to make him invincible, but his right heel, where his mother was holding him, was not submerged, so this became his one vulnerable spot.

- Slighted by king Agamemnon (during the war against the Trojans), he refused to fight.

- His friend Patroclus, put on Achilles' armour and was killed by Hector (Trojan hero).

- Achilles chased Hector around the walls of Troy three times, killed him, and dragged him behind his chariot around the walls of Troy.

- Paris shot an arrow that pierced Achilles' vulnerable heel, and killed him.

Adonis

- God of vegetation.
- A king was tricked by his daughter into an incestuous assignation. When her father realized, he sought to punish her, but she was rescued by the gods and turned her into a myrrh tree. Adonis was born nine months later, from the trunk of the tree.
- Aphrodite fell in love with the youth and sought to protect him from the wild animals of the forest. When he attempted to kill a wild boar he failed and was killed. Aphrodite, in an effort to immortalize her lover, sprinkled nectar into his spilt blood, from which flowers sprouted.

Aphrodite

- Goddess of beauty and sexual love.
- Daughter of Zeus. Conceived from the foam of the sea and Uranus' castrated genitalia.
- Mother of Eros and Hermaphroditus (a being of both sexes).
- She loved, primarily, Ares and bore him three children.

Apollo

- God of music, medicine, poetry and the fine arts, light and truth. Sun god. Oracle.
- Son of Zeus. Twin brother to Artemis.
- Considered the most beautiful of the gods.
- He was also very jealous of his talents and would punish severely anyone questioning them.
- Athena crafted a flute to play, but because she had to distort her face when she blew into it, she threw it away. A Satyr (called Marsyas) found it, taught himself how to play and eventually was so proficient that he challenged Apollo to a musical contest. The nine Muses were to be the judges. Apollo won the contest and, to punish the Satyr for his impudence, Apollo tied him to a tree and flayed him alive.

Arachne

- Lydian girl, very skillful in weaving and spinning.
- Challenged Athena to a contest .

- Depicted scenes of the gods at their worst - revealing all their weaknesses and bad habits. - Athena, angered by this, touched Arachne on the forehead to force her to recognize her guilt.
- Arachne went away to hang herself.
- Athena, however, had other plans for the presumptuous girl - she changed her into a spider and made her and her descendants "hang" forever.

Ares

- God of War.
- Little liked by the rest of the Olympian gods.
- In love with Aphrodite.
- "Caught in the act" for all the gods to see - embarrassed, they fled to distant parts of the earth. (Hence, Love and War are considered opposites).
- After being wounded during the Trojan War, Ares complained to Zeus about the injury - he was thus considered a coward and was forbidden to return to the fray.

Artemis

- Goddess of the hunt, chastity, marriage and childbirth, human rights, and the moon.
- Virgin, twin sister to Apollo.
- Moments after her own birth, Artemis helped deliver Apollo and from thence became the goddess of childbirth and the protector of children.
- Defender and avenger of rape victims.
- While bathing, naked in a stream, Artemis was discovered by a hunter called Actaeon. Having taken a vow that no one should ever see her naked, she punished the hunter by turning him into a stag. He was devoured by his own hunting dogs.
- Fell in love with a young shepherd called Endymion, who had been granted eternal youth and beauty, so long as he remained asleep.

Asklepios

- God of medicine
- Son of Apollo.
- Taught by Chiron the Centaur.

- The sign of Asklepios was the snake curled around a staff and this is still used for the more traditional medical practises today (as opposed to the caduceus of Hermes).
- His daughter, Hygeia, followed in his footsteps and became the female counterpart of the healing god.
- When Hades became jealous of Asklepios' power to raise the dead, he sought Zeus' help in having the healer destroyed. Zeus sent a thunderbolt to kill Asklepios, but then made him a god.
- Temples and gardens were erected in honour of Asklepios, where the sick, fatigued or anxious populace could receive mystical/miraculous treatment.

Athena

- Goddess of wisdom, arts/crafts, inventions and War
- Virgin.
- Born fully-grown and armed, from the head of Zeus.
- Accredited the invention of the yoke, the plough, the rake and the bridle, as well as the flute, trumpet, mathematics, clay pots and homemaking skills!
- Attacked by her half-brother Hephaestus, and from this attempted union sprouted the statues of Athens. (Another version holds that a being, half snake, half human was produced).
- The definitive symbols of Athena are her tall helmet, her shield with the head of Medusa in the centre, and her snake-rimmed cloak called an Aegis.

Centaurs

- Half man, half horse.
- At the wedding of the king of Thessaly, the centaurs got drunk and attempted to force their attentions on the new bride. Soon they were under attack by a tribe of locals called the Lapithae. Many centaurs were killed.
- The most famous of the (good) centaurs was Chiron, who was the teacher of Diomedes (Jason) and Asklepios.
- When he died, Zeus put him amongst the stars as the constellation Sagittarius.

Chaos

- The universe spawned from a great abyss with no form and which was in constant flux.

- Chaos gave birth to primeval darkness (Erebus), night (Nox) and lust (Eros).
- Nox and Eros gave birth to Love, who ruled the universe.
- Love gave birth to Day & Light and these siblings created Gaea (Earth) and Uranus (Heaven).

Charon

- Ferryman on the River Styx in the Underworld.
- The dead were supplied with money (in the mouth or on the eyes) to pay Charon to take them over to the gates of Hades.

Croesus

- King of Lydia (6th Century B.C.E.) - richest man of his time.

Damocles

- A courtier who over-praised the happiness of Dionysius the Elder (4th Century B.C.E. tyrant of Syracuse, Italy)
- Forced to sit at a banquet, under a sword suspended by a single hair that he might learn the perilous nature of that happiness.

Daphne

- Wood nymph.
- Apollo and Eros were having a contest to see who was the better shot with the bow, when Eros spotted Daphne in the wood. He pierced her with a lead arrow which instantly turned her heart against Love. Then he pierced Apollo with a golden arrow and as soon as Apollo saw Daphne he fell madly in love with her. Apollo pursued Daphne, but she ran away from him through the wood. Daphne called out to her father, a river god, to help her, and so he turned her into a laurel tree.
- Apollo took the laurel wreath as his emblem and it was thenceforth used to crown victors and kings.

Delphi

- Site of Oracle of Apollo (Sibyls).

Demeter

- Goddess of vegetation
- Vowed that the earth would receive no new life until her daughter, Persephone, who was taken down into the Underworld by Hades, was returned.
- Zeus ordered Hades to let Persephone leave temporarily, but Hades tricked her into eating three pomegranate seeds - symbols of fertility and marriage. Persephone was thus bound to return to Hades every year, for three months, but could remain with her mother on Olympus for nine.
- Vegetation thus grew from spring until autumn, but was banished from the earth in winter.

Dionysus

- God of wine and intoxication and of animal life.
- Half mortal son of Zeus.
- Hera discovered the infidelity and tricked Zeus into revealing his full divinity to his lover, who died instantly. She had been pregnant and Zeus removed the unborn child from her womb (1st birth) and placed it in his thigh from where the baby Dionysus was later born (2nd birth). Hera plotted to destroy the child and lured him away to be torn apart and eaten by the Titans. The gods collected the body-parts and buried them - Dionysus was reborn from the ground (3rd birth).
- Zeus turned Dionysus into a goat and he was entrusted to a group of mountain nymphs. There he discovered the grape vine and the process of making wine.
- Came to be identified with the Theatre.
- Followers were ecstatic women called Maenads, who danced and ate raw animal flesh in the god's honour.
- Like the vine, he was said to die each year and return in the spring.
- Took the form of a bull, snake, lion, fawn and kid.

Echo

- Mortal storyteller who was another victim of Hera's jealousy. Thinking that Echo had been flirting with Zeus, she punished her by taking away her gift of speech, leaving her able only to mimic the last words of others.

112

- Fell in love with the youth Narcissus, but every time he spoke all he heard in reply was someone repeating his last word. He became impatient and at the last moment, as he began to leave, Echo leapt out from behind a tree and flung her arms around his neck. Narcissus pushed her away and ran off. Echo was heartbroken and it is said she wept until she died, not eating, wasting away, leaving only her voice behind.

Eros

- God of love
- Son of Aphrodite and either Hermes or Ares.
- He would shoot arrows into peoples' hearts to make them love or hate: Lead arrows induced hatred, golden ones love.
- Remained a dimpled cherub-like figure until he was given a brother, at which time he sprang into adulthood.

Fates

- Clotho, Lachesis & Atropos were the three daughters of Themis (Law) and were the counselors to Zeus. They were in charge of spinning the thread of human destiny and were supplied with scissors to cut it if they so desired.

Furies

- Alecto, Tisiphone & Megaera, the Furies punished with a secret sting those who escaped or defied public justice.

Gordian Knot

- An oracle had said that the new king of Phrygia would come in a wagon and a certain poor farmer had arrived in the town square on a wagon. He was declared king and in honour of the oracle Gordius tied up the wagon with an intricate knot.
- It was said that the person who could loosen the knot would rule all Asia. Many tried but failed.
- Alexander the Great cut the knot in two with his sword and proceeded to conquer the Asian world.

Graces, Three

- Goddesses of social interaction.
- Daughters of Aphrodite and Dionysus (or the daughters of Zeus and a Titan female called Eurynome).
- The youngest, Aglaia, gave speakers eloquence and presence, Euphrosyne gave parties and social functions laughter, and the eldest, Thalia, was also the Muse of comedy.
- Attendants on Aphrodite.

Hades

- God of the Underworld and of wealth.
- Often mistaken for Death (Thanatos), Hades is often portrayed as a dark being, cloaked in shadows, rarely venturing from his own kingdom.
- For three months of the year he ruled with his consort Persephone, whom he kidnapped and tricked into marriage.

Harpies

- Winged creatures whose torsos and heads were of women, but whose lower bodies were of vultures.
- On his quest to find the golden fleece Jason lands on an island inhabited by a prophet called Phineus, who had been punished by Zeus for being too accurate. They taunted Phineus every time he tried to eat, stealing his food, defecating on his table. The Argonauts helped Phineus destroy the Harpies.

Hera

- Goddess of the family, familial love and legitimate childbirth.
- Zeus' sister and wife.
- Best known for her fierce jealousy and punishment when she discovered Zeus being unfaithful.
- Some of the most famous of her rivals were *Europa* (Gk), who attempted to ride a tame bull, only to discover it was Zeus in disguise, who then took her to Crete, Leda, who also "fell" for Zeus, this time in the guise of a swan, and Io, whom Zeus transformed into a white cow to hide her from his vengeful wife.

Heracles

- Half-mortal son of Zeus.
- Hera planned to kill Heracles so she sent snakes to bite him in his crib. Heracles strangled the snakes and lived to be a strong, athletic and skillful demi-god.
- Hera later attempted to destroy him: she made him temporarily insane, during which time he killed his own wife and children.
- Although it was not his fault, Heracles felt guilty and went to the Oracle at Delphi for advice.
- He was told that he could be cleansed of this deed only if he completed twelve years of service to his weak and disliked brother, the king. He completed Twelve labours.
- The lion-skin and the club are his signature possessions.

Hermes

- Messenger of the gods, god of business and commerce, rhetoric and the misleading sentence, and trickery. Guide of the dead.
- Son of Zeus.
- In the few moments it took for his mother to compose herself after giving birth to him in a cave, Hermes grew to boyhood and left in search of adventure.
- He stole some cattle from Apollo and used their guts to make strings for a lyre. On being discovered, Hermes gave Apollo the lyre as an apology and this soon became Apollo's signature instrument.
- Common symbols are the caduceus, which was his golden staff, and his winged shoes.

Hestia

- Goddess of fire/hearth and patroness of the six priestesses.
- Punishment for mistreating a priestess or for letting the fire extinguish was severely punished.
- The fire was ignited by the rays of the Sun.

Icarus

- Son of Daedalus, the most famous artisan in Athens.
- Daedalus had killed his nephew, of whom he was jealous. He took Icarus and fled to Crete.

- After some trouble with the king on Crete Daedalus was made prisoner of the island.
- Daedalus planned to escape. Inspired by birds, the artisan constructed wings for himself and his son. They were made of feathers, held together with wax.
- Icarus started to fly ahead, going higher and higher. The closer he got to the sun, the quicker the wax in his wings melted - he fell into the sea and was drowned.

Janus

- God of portals (gates) and beginnings & endings
- Had two faces looking in opposite directions.
- The city doors were shut in peace time and open in times of war, so the god could come to the city's defense.
- The month of January is named after Janus, for it is at the end of one year and the beginning of another.

Jason

- A boy called Diomedes was growing up under the tutelage of a Centaur called Chiron, who eventually told him that he was of royal decent, and that his throne had been usurped by an evil uncle.
- Chiron called the boy Jason.
- When Jason set out to claim his throne, the ruling king was told by the Oracle that he should beware of a man wearing one sandal. There were two stories about Jason losing a sandal - in one, he lost it in a muddy river while carrying an old lady across, in another, he took it off himself when the strap broke.
- The king told Jason that he would give him back the throne if he found and retrieved the golden fleece of a flying ram that had been sacrificed to Zeus.
- Jason had the *Argo* built and gathered together a crew of such renown as Heracles, Orpheus, and the sons of Apollo, Hermes, Ares and Poseidon.
- Through many trials and adventures they succeeded in finding the fleece; Jason was eventually made king.

Kronos

- Ruler of 2nd generation of gods.
- Gaea and Uranus created the race of mighty Titans, of whom Kronos was the leader.
- In a dispute with their father, Kronos castrated Uranus and cast his genitals into the sea.
- Kronos married his sister, Rhea and became the ruler of the next generation of gods.

Laocoon

- High priest of Apollo who opposed the reception of the wooden horse into Troy and was consequently killed, along with his two sons, by huge serpents.

Luna

- (Roman) The Moon.

Medea

- Princess who was also a sorceress.
- Fell in love with Jason and kept him safe through his various adventures.
- When Jason left her for another woman, she had the lover killed, then she murdered her own children, burnt her palace down and flew away in her serpent-pulled chariot to marry the king of Athens.
- The subsequent stories of Medea are full of bloody deeds and cruelty.

Medusa

- Chief of the three Gorgons.
- Originally, Medusa was a beautiful woman who had dared to vie in beauty with Athena and, as a consequence, was turned into the hideous, serpent-haired creature.
- All who looked at her were turned to stone.
- Perseus, a son of Zeus, was sent to slay Medusa - he was given Athena's shield and Hermes' winged shoes to assist him. By reflecting her image off the shield, Perseus was able to cut Medusa's head off, which he then gave to Athena, who placed it in the centre of her shield.

Midas

- When King Midas offered hospitality to a drunken friend of Dionysus, he was granted a reward of anything he chose. He asked that everything he should touch be turned to gold. Dionysus, unable to convince Midas to change his mind, granted his wish.
- Eventually everything in the kingdom had been turned to stone, including all food and water.
- Midas was near starvation when he finally asked for the wish to be reversed. He was told to wash in a sacred river to wash away his greed and stupidity. He went to live in the countryside, poor but happy, and became a worshiper of Pan.

Minotaur

- Half man, half bull.
- Kept by King Minos of Crete in a labyrinth designed by Daedalus.
- Young women were regularly sacrificed to the monster, but a brave young man called Theseus made it his quest to rid the city of this beast.
- Minos' daughter had fallen in love with Theseus and helped him by providing him with a sword and a ball of string to mark his path through the labyrinth.

Mount Olympus

- Home of the gods.

Muses

- Nine daughters of Zeus.
- At first, referred to in the singular, i.e., "the Muse" but later received their own identities.
- Calliope (scroll & stylus) = epic poetry; Clio(scroll or set of tablets) = written history; Erato = erotic poetry; Euterpe (flute/lyre) = lyric poetry and rapturous music; Melpomene (tragic mask and *cothurnus* - a thick boot worn by actors) = tragedy; Polyhymnia (thoughtful and pious) = religious poetry and song; Terpsichore (lyre) = dance; Thalia (laughing mask) = comedy; Urania (globe) = astronomy.
- The muses were the mistresses of Apollo and their abode was on Mount Helicon, or with Apollo on his sacred mountain of Parnassus.

Narcissus

- Beautiful youth.
- Tired of hunting, Narcissus stopped to drink from a spring. As he leaned down to drink, he saw, and fell in love with, his own reflection. He became so besotted with the face in the water that he began to fade away for lack of food and sleep.
- Eventually he died. Echo, who still haunted the woods, saw his despair and when he uttered his final words, "Oh, youth, beloved in vain, farewell!" - she echoed back, "Farewell!"
- When the wood nymphs went to get the body of Narcissus, they found in its stead a yellow flower, bending toward the spring, where it was reflected. Thus, the small Narcissus flower was named.

Nemesis

- Goddess of retributive justice and revenge
- She especially targeted the proud and insolent.

Nike

- Winged goddess of victory.

Niobe

- On the occasion of the annual celebration in honour of Leto and her children Apollo and Artemis, Niobe, the Queen of Thebes appeared dressed in her finest clothes, asking the crowd why she, too, was not being honoured for she had borne fourteen children!
- Indignant Leto caused all Niobe's children to be killed and in her grief Niobe herself turned to stone, but her weeping never ceased.

Odysseus

- A brave warrior from Ithaca who had fought in the Trojan War and was on his journey home when Athena, angered at the desecration of her Temple at Troy, determined that no Greek would return home.
- Poseidon helped by creating huge storms that destroyed many of the Greek ships, or sent them off course.

- Odysseus had many experiences and encountered many strange beings including:

1. The Lotus-Eaters, a race who ate the fragrant flower and walked about in a stupor.

2. The Cyclops, Polyphemus, who lived in a cave. To escape, Odysseus gave wine to the giant, who then fell asleep, drunk - three sailors took a large stick and pierced the eye of the Cyclops. As he fumbled about trying to find the sailors, the men escaped by hiding under sheep's skins and crawling under the giant's legs.

3. The enchantress, Circe, who lived on an island and turned her lovers into animals. Hermes gave Odysseus a magical herb that would protect him from her spells. He stayed on her island for a year. She told Odysseus about the dead prophet who could help him get home.

4. The dead prophet who was coaxed up from the Underworld by the smell of the blood of many sheep, which it drank. He told the sailors to go to the island of the sun-god, but warned them not to touch the oxen there.

5. The Sirens, whose song was so seductive it lured sailors to their death on the rocks. Odysseus had to strap himself to his mast and put wool in the ears of his crew, so as to be sure they would not succumb.

6. The island of Helios, the sun god, where there lived the sacred oxen that pulled Helios' chariot. Forgetting the warning, the hungry sailors feasted on an ox. Helios sent a bolt of lightning to kill the sailors. Odysseus was the only survivor.

7. He was carried on the waves to an island ruled by the sea nymph, Calypso, where he stayed for some time. By now, Athena had forgotten her vendetta and was feeling sorry for Odysseus, so she sent Hermes to Calypso to tell her to help the sailor on his way.

- With a little more help from various females Odysseus arrived home nineteen years after he had left for Troy.
- Thinking Odysseus must have been dead, men of the city sought to marry Penelope, his wife, but she always believed her husband would return.
- She tricked her unwanted suitors by unravelling at night a tapestry she had sewn during the day; she had promised to choose a man when she had finished it.
- Odysseus returned, disguised as a beggar and entered the court with the other suitors.

- Penelope declared she would marry the man who could string her husbands bow (a feat none had managed before) and fire an arrow through twelve golden rings in a row.
- All the suitors attempted the task, but only the beggar, much to everyone's amazement, succeeded. When he had shot the arrow through the rings, he shot each one of the suitors as well! Thus ended Odysseus' odyssey.

Oedipus

- Son of Laius and Jocasta, rulers of Thebes.
- Abandoned at birth and reared in the court of Corinth.
- Later, the city of Thebes was afflicted by a monster called a sphinx - it had the body of a lion and the head of a woman. It would offer passers-by a riddle which they had to answer correctly if they wanted to pass, otherwise they were killed. When Oedipus approached the sphinx he was asked "What animal walks on four legs in the morning, two in the afternoon and three in the evening?" He answered correctly (can you guess?). The sphinx was so devastated that it fell from its high rock and died.
- Returning to Thebes, Oedipus unwittingly killed his father, became king, and married his mother. Upon discovering his true relationship to Jocasta, Oedipus blinded himself and later died in exile.

Orpheus

- Greek musician, said to have been the son of Calliope, the Muse.
- His music was said to charm trees and rocks into following him.
- When his wife, Eurydice, died, Orpheus decided to go to the Underworld to seek her. He convinced Charon to take him across the Styx to Hades, who granted him permission to take his wife home. He was told not look back at her as he left, but he did and Hades stole her back. He waited on the riverbank for seven days, but he was not allowed to return to the Underworld.
- He found that he could no longer play merry tunes - when he refused to play for a group of women, they became angry and stoned him to death. Orpheus finally returned to Hades and was reunited with his wife.

Pan

- God of shepherds and the countryside, and patron of light music.
- Son of Hermes. Half man, half goat.
- Fell in love with a nymph called Syrinx, but when he attempted to lay with her she escaped and all he could grasp in his arms was a bunch of river reeds. As Pan sighed, his breath passed through the reeds making a pleasant sound. He decided to bind them together to make an instrument in honour of his lost love - he named the pipes Syrinx, after the nymph.
- Pan, in Greek, means "all" and so this god became identified with all of Nature and later, with all of "pagan" religious observances.

Pandora

- The first mortal woman.
- Sent down to earth by Zeus as a punishment to man for Prometheus' theft of the divine fire.
- She brought with her a box which contained all the evils of the world (Painful Death, Suffering, Disease, Plague, Jealousy, Hatred, Envy Crime), but with Hope at the bottom. She was warned not to open it, but she was curious and did. Out came all the evils, but the lid was shut in time to save Hope.

Paris

- When a disgruntled goddess was not invited to a wedding, she decided to cause trouble. She threw into the midst of the gathering a golden apple inscribed, "to the fairest." Aphrodite, Athena and Hera argued over who deserved the apple, and eventually demanded an independent judge.
- Zeus ordered Paris to award the prize but each goddess offered Paris a bribe. Aphrodite won the prize by promising Paris the hand of Helen, wife of Menelaus, King of Sparta. . When Paris took Helen, the 10-year Trojan War was triggered.

Pegasus & Bellerophon

- Pegasus was the winged horse of Apollo and the Muses who sprang from the blood of Medusa when her head was cut off.
- He was/is the traditional symbol of poetic inspiration, for the blow of his hoof

caused Hippocrene, the fountain of inspiration, to spring from Mount Helicon.

- The hero Bellerophon was the only being who could tame the horse and he rode Pegasus in a battle against the monster Chimaera, whom he slew.
- When Bellerophon became too proud and presumptuous, trying to fly up to the heavens, Zeus sent a gadfly to sting the horse, which sent Bellerophon falling to earth. He wandered about, lame and blind and eventually died.

Phaëton

- Half mortal son of Apollo.
- Forced to prove his divinity, he asked Apollo if he could drive the sun-chariot for a day.
- The horses soon proved too powerful, however, and Phaëton lost control and sent the chariot careering off course. The land was scorched and many living things were killed (this "explained" the Sahara Desert). The sky was scorched, leaving a long scar to be seen at night (the Milky Way).
- Poseidon at last begged Zeus to put an end to the destruction. Zeus sent a thunderbolt to stop Phaëton in his tracks. He fell to earth, his hair on fire.

Phoenix

- (Egyptian) Embodiment of sun god.
- Lived for 500 years then consumed by fire of its own making.
- Rose out the ashes as a youthful bird.
- Symbol of Immortality/perseverance.

Poseidon

- God of the oceans, earthquakes, and horses.
- Brother to Zeus.
- Father of the Cyclops (one-eyed giant)(mother = Medusa) and other monsters.
- Reigned over Atlantis which displeased him. He destroyed it with an earthquake.
- He was one of the four chthonic gods - gods who controlled the forces of nature (the others being Zeus, Hades and Demeter).
- Symbolized by his trident, or three-pronged "spear."

Prometheus

- Titan attributed the creation of humanity from mud.
- At a feast with the gods, Prometheus tricked Zeus out of the best portions of meat and gave them to the mortals. When Zeus discovered he had been made a fool of, he declared that humanity would no longer be free from hunger, and that they could no longer have the use of fire to cook their meat.
- Prometheus, feeling guilty, flew to the sun to steal some of its fire and brought it down to the earth where he hid it in the stem of a fennel plant.
- For this audacious act Zeus punished Prometheus by having him chained to the Caucasus Mountains where every day an eagle, or buzzard, would tear out his liver. The wound would heal overnight and the episode would repeat the next morning. He was eventually released by Heracles.

Psyche

- Personification of the Soul.
- Psyche had married Eros but was told that he was a monster in disguise, and that she could free herself if she slay him while he slept.
- Awoken by her attempt, and angered that she should distrust him so, Eros flew away.
- She sought Aphrodite's help in winning him back, but was forced to undergo many humiliating tasks to prove her worth.
- The final of these was to go to Hades to fetch a box from Persephone containing the goddesses' beauty. Like Pandora, Psyche was warned not to open the box, but of course, she did. Inside was not beauty, but sleep - a Stygian (Styx) sleep that made her appear dead.
- Eros, feeling sorry for her, asked Zeus for mercy. Hermes was sent to fetch Psyche and she was brought up to Olympus where she was given a cup of ambrosia and was thus became immortal.

Pygmalion

- A sculptor who created a carving of a woman so life-like that he fell in love with her.
- He named her Galatea and went to the temple of Aphrodite to pray for some miracle that would

bring the statue to life.

- On his return home, Pygmalion kissed Galatea and she awoke, stepped off her pedestal, and returned his affection. They were married in the temple of Aphrodite.

Roma

- (Roman) The personification of Rome.

Romulus and Remus

- (Roman) Founders of Rome.
- Suckled by a she-wolf.
- Romulus killed Remus because he ridiculed the city walls.
- Romulus became first king of Rome.
- His wife was the only married woman to be carried off during the Roman rape of the Sabine women.

Satyrs

- Half goats, half men.
- Woodland spirits of virility.
- Attendants of Dionysus.

Sol

- (Roman) Sun god
- Another name for Apollo.

Tyche

- Goddess of Chance and of Plenty.
- After a battle between Heracles and a bull, Tyche found a broken horn on the ground, filled it with leaves, flowers and fruit and took it as her emblem. This became known as the Cornucopia or "horn of plenty."

Zeus

- King of the Olympian Gods.
- Kronos, fearing that he, like his father Uranus, would be overthrown, ate his first five children as they were born.
- The sixth was Zeus, whom Rhea, Kronos☐ wife, had hidden and replaced with a rock to fool Kronos.
- Kronos ate the rock and Rhea fled with her son.
- Taught by Metis, the personification of Wisdom, Zeus learned how to overthrow Kronos.
- Metis gave him a magic potion which would make Kronos vomit up his swallowed children and when the five angry siblings were returned to life they joined forces and fought with Zeus against Kronos.
- The war between the Titans (Kronos) and the Olympians (Zeus) began. Zeus was victorious - he castrated Kronos.
- The male children of Kronos cast lots for territory - Poseidon became ruler of the oceans, Hades ruler of the Underworld and Zeus ruler of everything else.
- He sat enthroned on Mount Olympus.
- Often symbolized by a thunderbolt or an eagle (though he took the form of many animals).

Greek - Roman Names

(Only those names which have Roman alternatives are listed)

Aphrodite - Venus	Hades - Pluto (Dis)	Odysseus – Ulysses
Ares - Mars	Hephaestus - Vulcan	Pan - Faunus
Artemis - Diana	Hera - Juno	Persephone – Proserpïna
Asklepios - Aesculapius	Heracles – Hercules	Poseidon – Neptune
Athena - Minerva	Hermes - Mercury	Rhea – Cybele
Demeter - Ceres	Hestia - Vesta	Tyche - Fortuna
Dionysus - Bacchus	Kronos - Saturn	Uranus - Coelus
Eros – Cupid	Leto - Latona	Zeus - Jupiter
Gaea - Tellus	Nike - Victoria	

"A metaphor is a thing you shout through."

Biblical Symbolism/Allusion

- In *Close Encounters of the Third Kind*, Richard Dreyfus is surrounded by little child-like beings - he holds his arms out to them and the scene is bathed in a white light. This is classic Jesus-figure symbolism.

- The verb "to babel" is thought to stem from the Genesis story of the Tower of Babel, where the language of its builders was confused. Hence, to babel means, to speak nonsense, etc.

- The fig leaves put onto statues and paintings of nude figures during the last few centuries was done so to "hide" their "shame," just as Adam and Eve had worn them when they discovered their nudity. Artist's saw no harm in painting the human form, but puritan rulers of the Church found the figures disturbing. By covering up the "naughty bits," they returned the figures to a familiar state - that of humility.

- To call someone a "Philistine" means that they are devoid of culture and indifferent to art, for the Philistines were a warlike race (from Philistia) who ravaged Jerusalem and destroyed everything. (Modern research has proved this to be an erroneous perception, but the term remains derogatory).

- The modern concept of the "millennium" actually comes from the Book of Revelation, where it is claimed that Satan will be bound for a thousand years, during which time the just will reign with Jesus. After this, Satan will be freed, will raise an army against the righteous and will be defeated. The T.V. show, *Millennium* played on this concept and uses biblical symbolism in almost every episode!

- The term, "forbidden fruit" refers to the fruit Adam and Eve were told not to eat.

- "Fire and brimstone" refers to the destruction of Sodom and Gomorrah and is usually used to describe the ferocious style of a preacher's sermon.

- "Pride before a fall" is (part of) a Proverb (16:18).

- "The writing's on the wall" refers to the account, in the Book of Daniel, of a phantom hand that writes a mysterious message on the wall during a great feast. Only Daniel can interpret the message, and it turns out to be an ill omen for the Babylonian kingdom.

- In the film *Phenomenon*, John Travolta plays a Christ-like figure who is misunderstood when he acquires "miraculous powers" - many of the scenes, such as the people crowding around him at the book fair, pleading with him to heal their children and show them "magic tricks," are common allusions to Jesus' short career.

➢ A "Jeremiah" is someone who is forever expecting the worst, or who goes on about doom in the future.

➢ A "Judas" is a traitor. "Thirty pieces of silver" is a common metaphor for betrayal.

➢ "We all have our cross to bear" refers to Jesus having to carry his own cross to the site of his crucifixion. When someone says it today, it means "we all have our own problems."

➢ *The Gift of the Magi* is an O'Henry short story about a couple each sells a treasured possession to buy the other a Christmas gift. An allusion to the Adoration of the Magi.

➢ A "doubting Thomas" is someone who doesn't believe something unless he see for himself.

➢ To say you "wash your hands" of someone or something is to emulate Pontius Pilate and to have nothing more to do with him/her/it.

➢ The Samaritans take their name from the parable of the Good Samaritan.

➢ Many medical clinics, etc., are named "Bethesda" after the healing spring mentioned in the Gospels.

➢ In the final scene of *The Omega Man*, Charlton Heston plays the character of the last "pure" man on earth - he (literally) gives his blood to save others, and dies in a Christ-like pose. Even the title contains the "Omega" symbol, the last letter of the Greek alphabet, used since the earliest days of Christianity to denote Jesus (usually in connection with the first Greek letter, *alpha*).

Biblical Stories

Old Testament

Genesis: The title of the first book of the Bible means "origin." The creation of the world is described as well as the creation of the Israel nation.

1. The Creation of the World:

A) God Makes the World in Six Days and Rests on the Seventh (Sabbath).

Wind blows across dark "void"

LIGHT (day 1)

SKY (day 2)

EARTH & SEAS & VEGETATION (day 3)

SUN & MOON (day 4)

ANIMALS & BIRDS (day 5)

HUMANS (day 6) ...God rests on the seventh day! (Wouldn't you?!)

B) Fall of Humanity from Paradise

- Adam & Eve told not to eat fruit from the tree of the knowledge of good and evil.

- Eve is tempted by a serpent (Satan) to eat and she shares the fruit with Adam. (Original Sin).

- Immediately they become aware of their nakedness and their guilt and they try to hide their bodies with fig leaves.

- God finds out and has the couple banished from the Garden of Eden.

- Adam is forced to labour in the fields and Eve must suffer pain in childbirth. Humanity is "cursed" with Death.

C) The First Murder

- Adam & Eve's sons, Cain & Able, argue over the suitability of sacred offerings.

- Able, the younger brother, a shepherd, is devout and offers God his best sheep, but Cain is greedy and wants to keep the best for himself, so he offers God fruit instead.

- Cain's sacrifice is not considered "enough" by God, but Able's sheep offering is accepted.

- Cain becomes jealous of the "favourite" and kills him. He is banished.

D) The Deluge

- The earth is deemed corrupt by God and so he decides to destroy humanity. Noah, however, is found to be righteous and worthy of saving.

- God warns him to prepare a vast ship, called an ark, and on this he is to put a pair of each animal/bird he can find, along with himself and his family.

- All is destroyed, except the ark.

- Noah sends a dove out to seek for dry land - eventually it returns with an olive leaf in its beak, meaning land is near.

- Noah & his family and the animals repopulate the world.

E) Humans Scattered

- Noah's descendants migrate. They decide to build a city, with a tower reaching up to the sky.
- When God discovers that the people are working together well, with a single language, single idea, he gets worried and suggests that if he leaves them unchecked they will become too clever too quickly and will assume god-like traits.
- He scatters the people and forces them to speak in different languages so that they can no longer understand each other. Babel means "confused."

2. Creation of Israel:

A) Abraham

- God calls Abraham out of Ur in Mesopotamia.
- He is promised a land, called Canaan, for his descendants.
- He leaves with his wife, Sarah, and his nephew Lot.
- Eventually Abraham & Lot argue over the grazing land available and decide to split up. Abraham settles in Canaan, Lot goes to Sodom, on the banks of the Jordan River.
- Abraham & Sarah are childless. A surrogate, Sarah's maid, Hagar, is offered to Abraham and she bears a son, Ishmael. Sarah gets jealous and banishes Hagar.
- An angel assures the maid that her son will become the Father of the Arab tribes.
- Three angels visit their house, disguised as travellers, prophesying that they will have a son, called Isaac, despite their advanced age.
- Abraham ordered by God to sacrifice his only son. He obeys, but at the last minute a ram is substituted (by God) and Isaac is spared.
- Isaac marries Rebekah.

B) The Destruction of Sodom

- The angels who have visited Abraham are on their way to Sodom, to herald its imminent destruction because of its evil ways.
- The angels enter Lot's house and warn him to flee with his family.
- The city is destroyed with "sulphur and fire" as the family flees to the hills.
- They are warned not to look back toward the city, but Lot's wife does and she is instantly turned into a pillar of salt.
- Lot and his two daughters escape to a cave.

- They believe they are the only remaining humans on earth; the daughters get their father drunk and sleep with him so that they can conceive and repopulate the earth

C) The Twelve Tribes

- Isaac has twin sons, Jacob and Esau (firstborn).
- Jacob receives the blessing of the firstborn through mischievous means.
- He is sent to his father's homeland to find a wife and on the way he falls asleep. He has a vision of a huge ladder reaching from earth to heaven, with angels ascending and descending. Jacob declares this a holy site.
- He finds Rachel, watering her sheep by a well, and marries her.
- Jacob fights with an angel and is renamed "Israel."
- Their twelve children come to represent the twelve tribes of Israel.

D) Joseph in Egypt

- Youngest son of Jacob, and "favourite."
- He is awarded the special "coat of many colours," and this makes his brothers jealous.
- They throw him down a well, put animal blood on his coat and take it to Jacob claiming the boy has been killed.
- The brothers sell Joseph into slavery. He ends up in Egypt, the successful and wealthy servant of an officer.
- He is falsely accused of attempting to rape the officer's wife, and is imprisoned.
- Joseph has a gift for interpreting dreams. He interprets the Pharaoh's dreams correctly he is granted special status and eventually he rises to become the Pharaoh's right hand man.
- He meets up with his brothers again and forgives them.
- He makes it possible for his family to enter Egypt and escape a local famine.
- He is later known as the father of the northern tribes.

Exodus

- This title means "departure" and the book tells the story of the departure of the Israelites from their "captivity" in Egypt.
- The baby Moses is put into a basket and sent down the Nile in order to escape an order for every Hebrew boy to be killed (the Pharaoh thinks there are too many Hebrews in his land).

- The boy is found by the Pharaoh's daughter and is brought up as an Egyptian in the royal court.
- Moses later commits a murder and is on the run.
- While he is on a mountain, hiding, he is visited by God, in the form of a burning bush and a disembodied voice. He is told to return to Egypt to rescue the Hebrews from slavery.
- He meets up with his "brother," Aaron, and together they return to face the Pharaoh. God grants them the power to perform prophetic signs which are supposed to make the Pharaoh give in to their request, but after nine plagues of various types, they are still unsuccessful.
- The tenth plague, the "Death of the Firstborn," is the worst. The Hebrews are told to smear blood from a lamb over their own doors so that Death will pass them over. (Passover).
- The Pharaoh's eldest son is amongst the first to die - he orders the Hebrews to leave Egypt.
- The Egyptian army follows them. At the Red Sea, the waters are miraculously parted and the Hebrews walk across to safety. The Egyptians are drowned.
- The Hebrews spend forty days & nights in wilderness, being guided by a "divine" fire at night and a pillar of cloud during the day. God gives food from sky (Manna) and water from rocks.
- Moses is told to raise up a bronze serpent to save the people from death by snakebite.
- Moses goes on top of Mount Sinai and receives 10 Commandments written on stone tablets.
- The people make a golden calf - an idol. Moses breaks tablets in disgust, but later returns to the mountaintop to get another copy!
- A new priesthood is inaugurated & the tabernacle (extravagant tent used as mobile temple) is built to house the Ark (which holds the sacred stone tablets).

Joshua

- Joshua, Moses' successor, leads his people to the Promised Land.
- Spies are sent into Jericho, but they are where they are hidden in the house of Rahab, the prostitute.
- The Israelites march around the city for six days, on the seventh they march around it seven times and blow their horns.
- The walls collapse; Jericho's inhabitants (except Rahab) are killed.

Judges

- During the early settlement of Canaan, the Israelites are seen to adopt local/pagan gods and this angers the Israelite god, Yahweh. Eventually "judges" are sent to put Israel back on the right path.

A) Deborah

- Prophetess who seems to have authority and influence.
- Becomes actively involved in a war with the Canaanites.
- Canaanite general seeks refuge in a small town he thinks is neutral, but Jael, a woman living there, invites him into her tent and kills him with a mallet and tent peg. She is given honorary Hebrew status.
- Victory hailed in Song of Deborah.

B) Samson

- Phenomenal strength and personal "vendetta" against Philistines (Israelite archenemies) make him a legend in his own time.
- His strength is supposed to be in his hair and when he is asleep his lover, Delilah, cuts it off.
- He is captured and tied between two pillars beneath the Philistine Temple. In a last heroic gesture he pushes the pillars over and the Temple crashes down on him and the Philistines.

Ruth

- Moral and political story of matriarch of the house of David.
- Moabite daughter-in-law of Naomi.
- Famine forces the women to leave Moab - their men have died and they have no means of support.
- Ruth refuses to leave Naomi.
- She works hard in the fields and soon comes under the patronage of a kinsman, Boaz.
- Ruth behaves admirably under duress and proves to be a good Hebrew. She marries well and her descendants become the House of David.

1 & 2 Samuel

- Continuing history of the Israelites:

A) Samuel & Saul

- Samuel placed with priests for training and found to be one who is called for a special task.

- Many years later, the Israelites decide they want a monarchy, but God warns them against this. Eventually God gives in and he sends Samuel to find and elect Saul as the first King of Israel.
- Saul is troubled by many things and he instructs the young shepherd boy, David, son of Jesse, to play music for him.
- Samuel has already been told by God to anoint David as Saul's successor.
- Before a battle with the Philistines, Saul uses the outlawed services of a medium in order to decipher God's will (The Witch of Endor).
- The young David kills Goliath, the Philistine, with one rock from a slingshot.
- Saul becomes jealous of David's popularity and tries to kill him but fails.
- Saul eventually kills himself.

B) David

- David becomes king of Judah (southern tribe), then becomes king of all Israel.
- Commits adultery with a married woman, Bathsheba.
- Punished with death of firstborn.
- Has another son, Solomon.
- David is not granted permission by God to build a Temple in Jerusalem.
- Jewish Messiah said to come from house of David.

1 Kings

- Political History:

A) Solomon

- Effects multiple political marriages, notably with daughter of Egyptian pharaoh and other "foreigners."
- Builds Temple in Jerusalem.
- Founds vast, international trading establishment - the Queen of Sheba is thought to be one of his more extravagant trading partners.
- Known as Father of Israelite Wisdom. Most celebrated example being the decision to cut a baby in half to satisfy the petitions of two women, each claiming motherhood.

- Various unpopular practises marred an otherwise successful and peaceful reign - he used enforced labour to build Temple and raised taxes to finance it, etc. He attempted to unify the tribes, unsuccessfully, and the Kingdom broke up after his death.

B) Prophet & Harlot

- During subsequent reign of King Ahab, the prophet Elijah foretells serious consequences for the king's "ungodliness."
- Ahab is married to the "pagan" Jezebel, who worships the god Baal. She is intent on replacing the Israelite religion with her own, Canaanite cult and will stop at nothing to do so.
- Elijah performs miracles to demonstrate the greater power of Yahweh.
- King and queen die ignominiously - Jezebel is thrown from a high window and is devoured by dogs.

Esther

- The only book in the Bible not to mention "God," this is a tale of political intrigue and bravery. A tale of the history of Israel.
- A Persian king orders Vashti, his queen, to present herself before his dinner guests, to show off her beauty. She refuses and is deposed.
- The king searches for a new queen; Esther, a Jewish woman, is chosen.
- Mordecai, Esther's uncle, discovers a conspiracy against the king and tells Esther to alert him.
- The king's right hand man, Haman, is jealous of Mordecai's success in court and plans his revenge by conspiring to kill all Jews.
- Esther is again told to warn the king, but she is scared of revealing that she is Jewish. In the end she saves the day and all is well. Haman is hung, Mordecai given office and the Jews are allowed to take revenge. (Purim = Feast in her honour).

Job

- A philosophical tale of presumption, faith and patience.
- God allows Satan to test Job's faith.
- He suffers various misfortunes including loss of family, crops and health.
- Three friends come to offer sympathy; they discuss the subject of divine justice.
- Jobs protests his innocence and refuses to blame God for his troubles.

- God eventually speaks to Job, claiming it is impossible for humans to understand the ways of the divine. Job is humbled.
- All is restored and Job ends up with more happiness & prosperity than before.

Proverbs

- The proverbs are attributed to Solomon and are known as "Wisdom Texts."

    They tend to be very simple examples of common sense advice on how to live well, how to be wise and how to be devout.

Song of Solomon

- (Song of Songs, or Canticles) A non-Hebrew woman enters the court of a Hebrew King and rises from the status of "prostitute" to that of Queen. Erotic language.

Prophets (Isaiah, Jeremiah, Ezekiel, Daniel)

A) Isaiah

- The Lamb of God (said, by Christians, to foreshadow the coming of Jesus).
- The Suffering Servant (same sort of thing).
- People of Zion to triumph over an evil world.

B) Jeremiah

- The prophet stands at the gates of the Temple, warning the Jewish people that they will suffer for their iniquity.
- A redeemer from the line of David to restore Israel.

C) Ezekiel

- The visionary prophet.
-   Visions of the valley of bones, and the four-headed flying craft.

D) Daniel

- Interpretation of dreams; the "writing on the wall" at the feast of Belshazzar (Babylonian king).

- "Miraculously" escapes death in the lion's den when thrown in by the Persian king Darius for praying when a law had been passed prohibiting "commoners" to pray for a period of thirty days.

Jonah

- A tale of humility and obedience.
- Jonah is sent by God to convert the Assyrians of Nineveh.
- To evade the commission he sails to Tarshish but his ship is threatened by a great storm. By lot the blame falls on Jonah and he is thrown into the sea.
- He is consumed by a great fish, and stays in its belly for 3 days/nights.
- He repents and is freed. He resumes his commission.
- When his conversion of the Assyrians is successful and God begins to show favour to them, Jonah is angry with God and goes to sulk in the shade of a gourd plant. This withers and Jonah is exposed to the sun. This is a lesson to him from God - he is humbled.

Judith

- A story of the history of Israel.
- Set amid a complicated battle scene, involving the famous Babylonian king, Nebuchadnezzar.
- Holofernes, the king's general, is sent to punish local Israelites for refusing to give their support.
- Judith, a widow in one of the besieged towns, argues against a Jewish surrender and tells her people to trust in God.
- Because she is beautiful, she is invited to dine with the Holofernes.
- She lures him into her own tent, gets him drunk and cuts off his head with his own sword. Needless to say, she is deemed a heroine.

You Should Also Be Familiar With...

Passover: Feast to commemorate the Exodus from Egypt.

Apocrypha: Written texts not in the Jewish canon.

Covenant: Pact. God made several with the Hebrew nation - usually to do with land and descendants.

Diaspora: Scattering of Jews beyond Holy Land.

Idolatry: Worship of idols/gods not permitted in Judaism.

Jehovah: Pronunciation of YHWH, the "unutterable" name of Hebrew god.

Messiah: Traditionally a descendent of King David who would usher in a new age of peace and prosperity for Israel.

Rabbi: Jewish spiritual teacher.

Sabbath: Seventh day of week, commemorating Exodus. Holy day.

Torah: The first five books of the Old Testament, otherwise known as the Pentateuch. The teachings of Torah.

Cherubim & Seraphim: Angels of eighth and ninth order (9 orders). Seraphim have three sets of wings.

New Testament

The Gospels

There are four Gospels: Matthew, Mark Luke and John. The authors of these texts are called evangelists (or "teachers/preachers"). They are symbolically depicted as a man, lion, ox and eagle, respectively.

Infancy Stories

- Mary, a young virgin, is told by the Archangel Gabriel that she will conceive a son and will name him "Emanuel." (Annunciation).
- Joseph, a middle-aged carpenter, is Mary's betrothed.
- Hearing that she is pregnant, he plans to break off the engagement, but he is told by an angel that the conception is God's doing, not hers. He agrees to marry her.
- Elizabeth is Mary's elderly relative (not specified) and she also conceives a son through "miraculous" means.
- Elizabeth's son is John the Baptist. When Mary visits Elizabeth for the first time after the Annunciation, Elizabeth pays homage to Mary and her child in a prayer/song called the *Magnificat*.

- Jesus is born, according to tradition, in a stable in Bethlehem, where Mary & Joseph have to stay when they return to Bethlehem for a Census.

- Three Wise Men (Magi: magician-like Persian priests) see a portentous "star" in the East and they visit King Herod the Great to ask him where they can find the child who is to be "king of the Jews."

- Herod, the current king of the Jewish nation, feels threatened, so he tells the Magi to let him know when they have found the boy, so that he can honour him. This is a trick.

- The Magi follow the star, which seems to stop over Bethlehem. When they arrive, they find Mary & Joseph tending the baby, Jesus, in the stable. The men bring with them precious gifts - gold, frankincense and myrrh. They are warned in a dream not to return to Herod.

- In response to being tricked by the Magi, and in fear for the security of the kingdom (and the *status quo*), King Herod the Great orders to be killed all boys under the age of two, in and around Bethlehem.

- Joseph is told (in a dream) to take his family into Egypt, where the boy will be safe. Later, he is told (again in a dream!) to return to Israel, for Herod has died. The family settles in Nazareth.

- When Jesus is 12 years old he goes missing for three days and is later found sitting with the teachers, listening and asking questions. He explains to his parents that he is preparing to do God's work.

- Joseph educates Jesus as an apprentice carpenter.

John the Baptist

- Forerunner of Jesus. John, the son of Elizabeth and a Jerusalem priest called Zechariah, rejects his luxurious life, replaces his fancy clothes with camel-hair rags and goes to live in the wilderness.

- Preaching the need for redemption and baptizing people in the River Jordan, he heralds the coming of the Messiah.

- He baptizes Jesus, whom he declares is the Messiah.

- Openly opposes marriage of the Galilean tetrarch, Herod Antipas & Herodias.

- Herodias' daughter, Salome, dances at Herod's birthday dinner and makes the drunken king promise her anything she wants.

- She and Herodias conspire to request the head of John the Baptist on a plate.

- She is granted her request and John is beheaded.

Miracle Stories (most common)

A) Marriage at Cana

- Jesus, his mother, and some of his disciples are invited to a wedding.

- The wine runs out and Jesus is asked by his mother to provide more.

- He orders servants to fetch water in jars, he blesses it and by the time they pour it out it has changed into wine.

B) Calming the Storm

- Jesus is out fishing with his disciples and he falls asleep in the boat.

- A great storm arises and the men panic.

- They wake him up, fearing for their lives.

- Jesus tells the storm to stop and it does.

C) Walking on Water

- Jesus appears to his disciples who have taken their boat out into the middle of the Sea of Galilee.

- When one of the disciples (Peter) tries to imitate this act, he fails, and falls in.

D) Feeding Multitude

- Jesus takes a few fish and some loaves of bread and divides it between his disciples, who then pass it around to feed 5000 people.

- When all have had their fill there is more left over than was handed out in the first place.

E) Healing the Sick

- Jesus is said to make the lame walk, the blind see, etc. (Pool of Bethesda)

- He cures lepers and the "possessed."

- He is said to raise the dead. E.g., Lazarus is a young friend who apparently dies, but Jesus is said to call him out of his grave three days after burial.

Morality Stories

- On two or three occasions Jesus uses children as an example to his followers e.g., they are to become childlike (willing to learn, open-minded, humble, etc.) if they are to learn anything from him.

- In many instances, Jesus' followers are referred to as his children or as his sheep/flock. (Like Hermes before him, Jesus appeared in the guise of a shepherd and also as a "messenger" of the divine).

A) Sermon on the Mount

- Jesus teaches to crowds atop a mountain. The "Beatitudes" or blessings are spoken here.

B) Parables

- (Wise sayings, anecdotes, stories, etc., which teach a moral).

Good Samaritan: A man walking from Jerusalem to Jericho falls into the hands of robbers and is left on the side of the road to die. A priest and a Levite (devout Jews from Jerusalem) passed him by because they didn't want to come into contact with a dying man (for purity reasons). When a Samaritan (a resident of Samaria - a place Jerusalem is constantly at loggerheads with) comes across the bleeding man he helps him and pays for his care at a local inn.

Prodigal Son: A man divides his property between two sons. The youngest moves abroad and squanders his inheritance. When he is starving, he returns to his home, ready to repent for his foolishness. His father welcomes him with open arms, gives him new clothes and feeds him his best calf at a celebratory meal. "He was lost and is found."

C) Adulterous Woman

- A woman caught in the act of committing adultery (punishable by death) is brought before Jesus for judgement, but he refuses to condemn her.

Divinity & Kingship

A) Temptation

- Jesus is said to undergo three temptations before his ministry begins.

1. Satan tells Jesus, who has been fasting in the desert, that if he is truly the Son of God he should be able to turn stones into bread.

2. Satan puts Jesus on the pinnacle of the Temple and urges him to jump, in order to prove that he cannot be injured.

3. Jesus is taken up a mountain and is told that all he sees will be his if he worships the devil.

- Jesus overcomes these temptations and this is used as proof of his divinity.

B) The Twelve

- Twelve Disciples represent the twelve tribes of Israel.

C) Storming of the Temple

- Jesus gets angry with the people who seem not to care about keeping the Temple (his "Father's House") a sacred place - he overturns tables, throws money down and upsets the entire marketplace where animals are sold for sacrifice. Chasing the dealers out, with a whip in his hand, he attracts the attention of the authorities, and in some of the accounts this is ultimately why he is arrested.

D) Anointing

- Mary Magdalene, the prostitute whom Jesus befriends, anoints Jesus' feet with expensive oils and wipes them with her hair.
- Judas, the group's Treasurer, argues that the expensive oil could have been sold and the money given to the poor, but Jesus defends Mary and tells the disciples she is anointing him in preparation for his burial.

E) Transfiguration

- Jesus and his closest disciples go up a mountain to pray.
- Some of the disciples fall asleep, but they wake up to find him shining, dressed in white, and standing between two of his Old Testament forerunners, Moses and Elijah.
- A bright cloud hovers over them and from it is heard a voice, saying that Jesus is the son of God.

F) Entry into Jerusalem

- Jesus ceremoniously rides a donkey into Jerusalem.

- Christians see this as a symbolic gesture that implies Jesus is the expected Messiah. (i.e., citing Old Testament Texts as precedents).

G) The Last Supper / Washing of the Feet

- Jesus has a final meal, of wine and bread, with his disciples.

- In a symbolic gesture, Jesus compares the wine to his blood and the bread to his body.

- This becomes, in the Catholic Church, the foundation of the Sacrament of the Eucharist, later developed into the rite of eating the Host in Church.

- At this meal, Jesus washes the feet of his disciples to show them that all are equal, etc. Often seen as a sign of humility.

Betrayal, Arrest and Crucifixion

A) Judas

- At the Last Supper, Judas leaves to betray Jesus' whereabouts to the authorities.

- He receives 30 pieces of silver for his act.

- Jesus & the disciples go to the Garden of Gethsemane.

- As the disciples sleep and Jesus prays, Judas arrives with the arresting officers and, in order to identify Jesus to the soldiers, Judas kisses Jesus on the cheek.

- Judas hangs himself because he can't live with the guilt. He is seen as a "coward" and traitor.

B) Peter

- When Jesus is arrested, Peter curiously attacks the slave of the high-priest, called Malchus, cutting off his right ear - he is rebuked by Jesus for this act of violence.

- Peter doesn't go with the rest of the disciples when Jesus is taken away, but remains with the arresting officers, keeping warm by a fire.

- When he is asked, three times, by various people, whether or not he is also a disciple, he claims never to have known Jesus.

- Jesus had predicted this would happen, claiming Peter would deny him three times by the time the cockerel crowed.

C) Mockery

- After Jesus is arrested, he is subjected to severe beatings, lashes and the tormenting mockery of his captors.
- He is dressed in a purple robe, a crown of thorns is pressed onto his head, he is spat at and forced to pretend he is a "king."

D) Pontius Pilate

- The Roman procurator who is finally responsible for sentencing Jesus under Roman law, is best known for four things:
    1. His wife has a dream in which Pilate suffers the consequences of condemning an innocent man.
    2. He asks Jesus "What is Truth?"
    3. He offers to release one prisoner, when there is a choice of only two - Barabbas the thief is released and Pilate hands Jesus over to be crucified, saying "here is the man," or "behold the man."
    4. Pilate then washes his hands of the whole affair.

E) Crucifixion and Burial

- Jesus is forced to carry his own cross up to the hill known as Golgotha, where he is crucified with two other men, who are robbers.
- He watches as soldiers cast lots (dice) for his clothing.
- He says a few last words on the cross, including the famous phrase, "My God, my God, why have you forsaken me?"
- Joseph of Arimathea goes to Pilate to request the body and Jesus is taken down from the cross by his family and put in a tomb until the Passover is finished.
- Joseph of Arimathea and Nicodemus bring spices and oils to the burial site, and Jesus is covered with a burial sheet (presumed to be the Shroud of Turin).
- When the disciples go to retrieve the body on the third day, it is gone.

F) Resurrection

- Jesus is said to rise from the dead on the third day. (Easter)
- In some sources he does so in full view of the Roman guards posted outside his tomb.

- He appears to Mary Magdalene first, warning her not to touch him because he needs to remain "pure" until his work is finished.
- He appears to many of his disciples for some time afterward. He is said to go to heaven, to sit with his father, God.

Post-Resurrection Stories

A) Thomas

- Thomas, a disciple, is famous for his hesitancy in believing the stories that Jesus has "risen" from the dead, until he sees for himself.
- Jesus appears before him and tells him to touch the wounds inflicted during the crucifixion.
- Thomas does so and then believes.

B) Peter

- After Jesus' death, Peter becomes the leader of the Christian Church and travels the land preaching the Gospel and performing healing "miracles."
- He is eventually crucified, upside down, in Rome.
- It is he who is said to hold the Keys to the Kingdom and it is he who is said to stand at the gates of Heaven.
- He is called the "Rock" upon which Jesus is said to have built his Church.
- He is said to have been the first "Vicar of Christ" - the first Pope.

C) Paul

- Paul is a Roman Citizen whose Roman name is Saul, but he is also a Jew and a Pharisee (the main antagonists in the stories of Jesus).
- He has been threatening the disciples of Jesus with death because he sees them as troublemakers.
- On the Road to Damascus he is thrown off his horse when a blinding light fills the sky.
- The voice of Jesus is heard, asking Saul "why do you persecute me?"
- Saul is blinded for several days and is converted - he changes his name to Paul.
- He travels, preaching, and writes letters to first Churches, explaining the new Christian religion.

Book of Revelation (Apocalypse)

- There are too many concepts in this Book to discuss here, but some of the more familiar are:

1. The Book with Seven Seals

2. The Seven Candlesticks

3. The Four Horsemen

4. New Jerusalem coming down from the sky as a bejewelled city.

- The Book tells of a vision of the final Judgement, when good and evil battle it out and all sin, disease, death, war, famine, etc., will reach a climax and will then be conquered. Jesus will apparently return in triumph and a new age of peace and harmony will begin.

You Should Also Be Familiar With...

Catholic: Means "Universal"

Messiah: Jewish tradition held that a savior or redeemer of Israel (the "anointed one") would come from the house of David. He would destroy all Israel's enemies and a new age of peace, prosperity and devout worship would begin. Some believed Jesus was this redeemer, divinely sanctioned to "save" the nation. The term "Christ" is (generally speaking) the Greek equivalent.

Heresy: Anything spoken, written, etc., in contradiction of the tenets of the Catholic faith.

Inquisition: Authority set up to thwart heresy and punish heretics.

Crucifix: The cross of wood upon which Jesus was crucified, made into an icon for church decoration and personal use (e.g., on rosaries).

Transmutation: The alleged transformation of the Eucharist into Jesus' actual body (and of the wine into his blood) during the rite of Communion.

Sacraments: Seven sacred rites available to Catholics: Baptism, Communion, Confirmation, Marriage, Penance, Holy Orders and the Last Rites.

Martyrs: Those who suffer and/or die for their faith.

Purgatory / Indulgences: A place of temporary or permanent punishment, after death. Indulgences, which could earn you points against your time in Purgatory, were sold by the Church.

Saints: People whose devotion or selfless acts grant them a special place in "Heaven" - they are sanctified by God or by the Church.

Angels: God's messengers. Can appear in any form. Most familiar are Archangels Michael & Gabriel.

Reformation: Martin Luther pointed out certain arguments against the tenets of the Catholic faith. Founded Lutheranism, which later became known as Protestantism.

Parable: An allegory employed to teach a moral, etc. Jesus teaches in parables.

Good Shepherd: Jesus is often depicted as a shepherd protecting his sheep.

Gnosticism/*gnosis*: Mystic perception of the nature of God. "Knowledge."

logos: "word" - divine reason, Jesus is said to be the incarnation of the "Word."

"Second Coming" (Parousia): Jesus is believed to return at the end of the world, to "rescue" the righteous.

Madonna: Jesus' mother, Mary, said to have been immaculately conceived (no Original Sin).

Beloved Disciple: Jesus had one "favourite" disciple who is never explicitly named, but who is privy to Jesus' most intimate thoughts and actions.

Apostle: Disciples are considered to be any follower of Jesus and his religious movement. Some say the Apostles are those disciples who were *both* at the Last Supper *and* "witnesses" to the "risen" Jesus; others say they were the inner circle of twelve disciples, or that they were the first preachers of the gospel.

CHAPTER 11: THE CREATIVE FLAIR

What I would like to offer you now is a selection of thought-inspiring projects that you can try in your own time. The aim is to let your imagination get some exercise; where writing is the main project, use a brand new notebook, a new pen, and keep them only for doing these particular exercises, find a quiet place, and have some fun. The projects can be performed as many times as you like, using themes of your own choosing.

❖ Using the following sentence as a starting line and, timing yourself for thirty minutes only, write a short story:

In the corner of the room lurked a spider...

❖ Flip through a picture magazine or book until you find an image you like. Look at all the details, as we discussed earlier, and make up a story to fit the scene.

This image, for instance, shows two people with crossbows. Who are they? Are they historical figures, or "reconstructionists"? Are they preparing for a battle, or a tournament, or are they trying out the "goods" before they buy? Are they male or female? Provide a tale with a beginning, middle, and end, to shed light on these folk!

❖ Find a copy of Tennyson's poem "Ulysses," and, using the information given in the mythological section above, rewrite the account of the ageing mariner as if it were a newspaper article.

This means analyzing the poem, first. You need to know what is being said (you don't want to be sued for libel!), e.g., to whom is the old man directing his comments? Who is it that will take over while he is away? What do you think the effect will be on his people if he goes? Keep the sentences short-ish, and direct. Have fun with it, and decide whether it's going to be a tabloid "exclusive," or a serious investigation into the state of the nation!

❖ Find images of two different statues depicting David, separate a page into two columns, and list everything that is similar, everything that is different about these works. E.g., is one clothed, the other naked? Then, try to explain what effect these variation have on your attitude to, or interpretation of the statue.

Remember, there are at least four famous "David" statues: Michelanglo's, Bernini's, Verroccio's, and Donatello's. Each is unique. They cover the extremes, from innocent, almost effeminate youth, to contemplative, intense manhood. Which do you think best suits the David of the biblical story? Which is more pleasing, artistically?

❖ Write a formal sonnet on the theme of …wood, or plastic, or metal.

This can be quite fun, actually, though not as easy as it may sound. Sonnets have fourteen lines, and must be either of the Shakespearean, or the Petrarchan sort.

❖ Look through the local paper and find an article that really gets you annoyed! Prepare an argument against this article's conclusions, providing all the necessary support, etc.

Follow the guidelines set out in Chapter 7.

❖ Watch Kenneth Branagh's *Hamlet*!

I recommend that you watch this alone, the first time, with a trusted, like-minded friend the second, and with a group, the third! There is so much to take in, so take your time. Here's a little quiz to see how observant you are…

1. When Hamlet first makes his appearance, what is he doing?

2. What building is used for the setting of Elsinore (check the credits)?

3. What object does Hamlet "open" while he speaks in the library?

4. On what vehicle do Rosencrantz and Guildenstern arrive at Elsinore?

5. Where does Ophelia hide the key to her cell?

These are just a few...try some on other viewers!

❖ Keep a small notebook with you whenever you can, and in it write all the interesting snippets of information, potential quotations, "nice-sounding" words, etc.

Some of my favourites include:

"A book is like a garden carried in the pocket" (Chinese Proverb)

"I still miss my husband...but my aim is improving!"

"...thus decimated..."

Constable clouds

mesmeric

❖ Stick a pin in a map and write a paragraph or two describing what you would find there...even if it's in the middle of the ocean!

There, one might find a pod of whales, or a great rolling wave. The sky may be threatening, or clear, but it would seem huge. There may be a ship, or a convoy of ships, or maybe a raft with sailors on it. The sea may be grey, blue, or shimmering silver. Travel with the mind!

❖ Go to a synagogue, or a church, or a mosque - if you've never been to any, go to all three...if you've been raised in one religion, visit another. Don't be judgmental and always be polite. Just look around you, watch people discretely, ask questions if you can.

You don't have to be "religious" to appreciate other cultures, and this is a great way of meeting people when they're in a good frame of mind! I thoroughly enjoyed going to the synagogue for the first time, as I went with two of my sisters and we stayed for hours, talking to several people, and just listening to the fascinating discussions.

❖ Ask someone you think has probably read a lot and ask them to list their three favourite books...then check them out.

Mine are: **A Romance of Two Worlds**, *by Marie Corelli (which is about a Victorian woman in search of the secrets of electricity);* **Jude the Obscure**, *by Thomas Hardy, and, believe it or not,* **Harry Potter**...*yes!*

❖ Instead of watching television one night, put on some instrumental music (find some on the radio if you don't own any) and, assuming you are alone, or have invited the others to join you, turn the lights down low, close your eyes and try to imagine what inspired the composer to write what he did. It can be fast, slow, mournful, jolly, cultural or quirky, but the trick is to "hear" the meaning of the music...meaning, that is, to *you*. Some of you may recall the old "Music & Movement" lessons...it's a chance to be a kid all over again!

South American pan pipes are good for this, or Navaho music. I had to do M&M to Holst's Planet Suite, when I was about five!

❖ Go to a local café philosophy session and join in.

Often you have to pay a dollar or two, but it can be a very refreshing experience, especially if you have no one in your family, or home, to sharpen your debating skills on. No one will push you to join in, so if you're a bit shy, just sit back with a coffee and listen.

❖ Explain the difference between the following objects (yes, there IS a difference. Hint? Mythology):

❖ Suggest how these objects could be used symbolically:

❖ Experiment with haiku (if you are uncertain what this is, look it up!).

❖ Describe the sound of air and the smell of water. If you use abstract ideas, explain your reasoning.

*Someone once told me that she thought rainbows were noisy things. When I asked her why, she said "All those colours jostling for such a little strip of sky – it **must** be noisy!" She was six...now there's an imagination in the making!*

❖ Make a promise to yourself to investigate at least one new painting, poem, story, artist, musical composition, etc., each week, or each month.

This one's up to you.

❖ Visit your local museum, art gallery, etc., and decide on an exhibit you would like to know more about. Ask the docent, or the manager, if it is possible to get "behind the scenes" and see what has to be done to prepare such a display.

Choose a time that isn't too busy, and you may see things that have just come in and haven't even been catalogued yet, or maybe you could watch as a local "find" is cleaned and prepared for display. Offer yourself as a volunteer, perhaps.

❖ Choose a person from history - at least a hundred years ago - and write down everything you think you know about them. Then go an do some research. Plan how long you will allow yourself - two hours, say, and see how much information you can glean from every source. Details are best, one-line anecdotes, a few dates, etc. Did you know more than you thought you did? Were you surprised at how much you didn't know?

I did this with Michelangelo and Beethoven, and discovered so much more about their personalities, thoughts, and experiences – such knowledge makes me hear new things in the music, and see alternative aspects of the sculptures.

❖ Choose a fictional character from a book at least one hundred years old, and write "A Day in the Life of ..." - in diary form.

Here are some examples:

Tiny Tim from **A Christmas Carol**

Mr. Rochester from **Jane Eyre**

Montmorency (the dog) from **Three Men in A Boat**

❖ Collect famous quotations and start using them in your essays (e.g., I used to use a partial quotation as a title, or place a small block quotation at the very beginning of the paper). It must be pertinent, though!

❖ Audit a course you have been keen to investigate, but couldn't fit into your regular schedule. It won't matter if you miss some sessions.

This is a great project for exposing yourself to new topics, such as the philosophy of science, or mediaeval architecture. Remember, everything is linked to something else, so no course would be a waste of your time.

❖ Read a play that you have heard a lot about but have never seen performed. Take on one of the roles, and whenever you have lines to read, read them out loud, in character. Get a feel for the language, the mood, and the meaning of the scene.

*One of the best, I can think of, is Dylan Thomas' Under Milk Wood. It's tough, but so good!
Listen to a recording only after you've read it yourself.*

❖ Hang out with your instructors whenever possible - some of them can be mines of information,
   and they will gladly impart on you the wisdom of their experience, if you take the initiative.
   Sometimes it's a group discussion at a café, or an impromptu walk across campus
   together...experience and enthusiasm are the two most precious resources you should seek out.

"Queen Elizabeth was called the Virgil Queen because she knew Latin."

THE END

Once you have exposed yourself to every conceivable form of inspiration, have absorbed all the myths and stories, have memorized who wrote what, when, and can write the perfect paper...you will be superhuman. Don't worry - perfection is not the goal, here. The goal is self-improvement.

Being a "perfect" student means you have no room for betterment, and that is either sad, or a miracle. In my second-year English Literature course, my instructor admitted to me that I had been the only "A+" student she had taught in over five years...but she was sorry to have to tell me that an "A+" was not going to appear on my Statement of Grades. When I asked why, she, like the Philosophy professor who lowered my essay grade in the second year because I hadn't stretched myself mentally, told me that if she gave me such a mark, I would have "nowhere to go." That, she argued, was not the best thing for me. She was right.

Hopefully, reading this book has highlighted your strengths and weaknesses in the various areas, and has provided you with enough of a foundation to enter, or continue with, Humanities classes with new confidence.

If you have the will to excel, and you apply yourself to 80% of what is in this book, you *will* reap the rewards. Remember that no matter what area of the Humanities you set your heart upon, these techniques and ideas will serve as a cornerstone of your success; they can be applied to any topic, be it Post Modern American Literature or Mediaeval Architecture. You will always have to write essays, always have to prove your point, always have to analyze things...but there is absolutely no substitute for an inquisitive mind, so keep your curiosity levels high and your options open.

Choosing your major in the first year of university isn't necessary - sample what the world has to offer. Be expressive, and learn how to defend your choices, be they choices of vocabulary, concept, or action. If you cannot defend them, rethink them - perhaps you are on a path that will not fulfil you in the long run.

Being the best student you can be, especially in a particular field that delights and inspires you, is one of the most satisfying goals, for it teaches you to challenge your own limitations, seek knowledge beyond that offered by the "system," and appreciate the rich diversity of human endeavour.

I wish you luck!

Other Tripping Lightly Books
By Janet Tyson

Our Man In Judea
The Secret World of the First Gospel

The quest for the historical Jesus is about to take a quantum leap!
The most controversial, intriguing, and realistic account of the man who dared to challenge the status quo...

ISBN: 0-9689912-1-1
376 Pages / 6 x 9 Paperback / $22.95 US

Available anywhere fine books are sold, or contact Tripping Lightly at trippinglightly@hotmail.com

Coming Soon !!!

Unravelling the mysteries of the most famous "love poem" in history...

The Song of Solomon

Why has there been constant debate over the Song's place in the canon?
Why is it so erotic?
Did Solomon write it?

The answers may surprise you!

Anticipated publishing date: Spring 2003

Printed in the United States
4376